D1229821

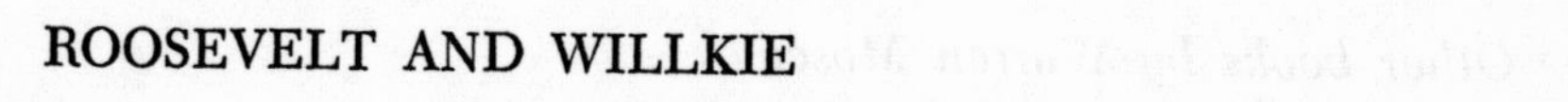

ROOSEVELT AND WILLKIE

Other books by Warren Moscow

WHAT HAVE YOU DONE FOR ME LATELY?

POLITICS IN THE EMPIRE STATE

ROOSEVELT AND WILLKIE

by

Warren Moscow

Prentice-Hall, Inc., Englewood Cliffs, N.J.

All photographs by World Wide Photos.

ROOSEVELT AND WILLKIE by Warren Moscow

Library of Congress Catalog Card Number: 68–21139

Printed in the United States of America

T

Prentice-Hall International, Inc., London
Prentice-Hall of Australia, Pty. Ltd., Sydney
Prentice-Hall of Canada, Ltd., Toronto
Prentice-Hall of India Private Ltd., New Delhi
Prentice-Hall of Japan, Inc., Tokyo

This volume is respectfully dedicated to the late James Andrew Hagerty, who for the half-century between 1910 and 1960 was the best political reporter there was.

Author's Note

It was my good fortune as a political reporter to be assigned to cover the national political conventions from 1932 through 1952, which includes the period of the first nomination of Franklin D. Roosevelt and the first nomination of Dwight D. Eisenhower, and also to work on the political campaigns which followed the nominations. To me and I believe to others of the same political generation, the 1940 situation—the conventions and campaigns of both parties—was the most fascinating of all, and I felt that someday it should be the subject of a book.

Countless millions of words have been written about Roosevelt and the beginning of America's participation in World War II, and a growing number about Willkie. This volume is an attempt to tell of the 1940 contest as a single coherent piece from the viewpoint of national politics. As far as I know, it is also the first attempt to detail the real background of Willkie's nomination, which at the time was either oversimplified or made unduly mysterious.

Most of the information is of my own gathering, rather than the product of research in other writings. Some I collected at the time when it was happening, some as I began talking with men and women who had been important factors, preparatory to writing.

I owe much to many who helped. In no particular order, they include:

John D. M. Hamilton, former chairman of the Republican National Committee, whom I have known since the 1936 campaign and who gave freely of his time and recollections.

Samuel F. Pryor, Jr., one of the early pro-Willkie men.

James P. Selvage, an Old Guard Republican friend of long standing, former publicity director of the Republican National Committee.

Fred Smith, another public relations pro, who helped organize the preconvention publicity drive for Willkie.

Harold J. Gallagher, Willkie's former law partner.

J. Russell Sprague, former Republican National Committeeman from New York, who headed up Dewey's 1940 drive for the nomination.

James A. Farley, former Democratic National Chairman.

Frank Altschul of Lazard Frères.

Mrs. Charlton MacVeagh and Charlton MacVeagh, Jr., widow and son of the man who sparked the Willkie nomination drive from behind the scenes.

Arch N. Bobbitt, chairman of the Indiana delegation to the 1940 Republican convention.

Albert Mark, public relations director of the Democratic National Committee.

Gertrude Hess Parker of the New York County Republican Committee.

Professor Karl A. Lamb of the University of California, Santa Cruz, who has done extensive research into the politics of this era.

Frieda Chait, of the New York City Municipal Reference Library.

Lamoyne A. (Lem) Jones, once a reportorial competitor, who filled me in on things that only he, as Willkie's press secretary, could know.

AUTHOR'S NOTE

The list of those who helped me accumulate the facts back in 1940 is far too long for inclusion, even if I could be sure of recalling them all. I do think back with fondness of the ushers in the Philadelphia convention hall who allowed me to sit in on the Michigan delegation caucus which assured Willkie's nomination and of the equally anonymous electrician at the Chicago Stadium who tipped me off how to trace the "voice from the sewer" attempting to stampede the Democratic convention for Roosevelt.

For readings to refresh my memory, and to find documents otherwise difficult to locate and copy, I used:

Jim Farley's Story, James A. Farley, Whittlesey House, New York, 1948.

Roosevelt and Hopkins, Robert E. Sherwood, Harper & Brothers, New York, 1948.

Working with Roosevelt, Samuel I. Rosenman, Harper & Brothers, New York, 1952.

Wendell Willkie, Fighter for Freedom, Ellsworth Barnard, Northern Michigan University Press, Marquette, Michigan, 1966.

Microfilm copies of *The New York Times,* 1939 and 1940.

None of the people with whom I talked is to be held responsible for the conclusions I have drawn. Those are strictly my own.

WARREN MOSCOW

New York

TABLE OF CONTENTS

ROOSEVELT AND WILLKIE

1 The Overture

Every fourth year presidential campaigns inevitably roll around, presenting new issues and usually new rivals. They hold the interest of the American people, for a time, to an extent unchallenged by any other regularly scheduled event. The contest in 1940 between Franklin Delano Roosevelt as the Democratic Party nominee and Wendell L. Willkie as the Republican stands out as a star attraction in a century of such elections.

The 1940 campaign competed successfully for world attention against history-making headlines shouting the military and diplomatic victories of a German madman over most of the world familiar to Americans. As the months passed by the political and military news merged. It became harder and harder to draw the line at which the political news ended and the war news began.

England stood alone as the last important democracy in the way of total domination of Europe by dictatorships. Few believed she could continue to resist unaided. Americans envisaged the loss of the British fleet as their Atlantic safeguard and uneasily conjectured the eventual invasion of America and the destruction of our form of government. Thus the war in which America was not yet engaged came far closer to home for the voters than it had, for example, in 1916—the previous prewar election year—or even during the 1952 campaign and its Korean War.

Apart from its immediate political result—the re-election of Roosevelt—the 1940 campaign had aftermaths of great and lasting consequence.

America in 1940 was still suffering from the effects of the Great Depression, and only the emergence of defense industries eliminated the chronically high rate of unemployment. Deficit financing by government was decried rather than accepted as necessary; the privileges granted organized labor under the still new Wagner Act were revolutionary to business executives. One result of the 1940 election was to firmly implant the New Deal as the Democratic Party philosophy, rather than Roosevelt's personal one.

On the Republican side, the 1940 campaign saw the creation of the Eastern Establishment, that loose collection of publishers, bankers and intellectuals which was to control every future Republican convention until the Nixon convention of 1960.

Finally, the personalities of the two candidates in 1940, and the circumstances under which they were nominated, fixed America's role in World War II and affected the thinking and postures of both major parties in world affairs for a quarter-century that followed, centering about a global-oriented bipartisan foreign policy.

The election results were not even close, nor, in retrospect, should they have been difficult to predict. Yet at the time the contest produced a tenseness, a feeling of thunder in the air, that still makes it memorable to those who participated. It brought out to the polling places men and women who never before had bothered to come, and many an experienced voter tossed restlessly at night over the responsibility of his vote. His nightmare was that his vote alone would turn out to have determined the result.

There were two major issues, the war and the home front. Though each candidate argued his own election was the best guarantee of keeping America out of war, few believed it could be accomplished by either at that stage of affairs. Both candidates and both parties had taken firm anti-Hitlerian positions, had already made America a *de facto* ally of Britain by pledging her all aid short of war. Both parties and both candidates contradicted their unneutral positions by other pledges that they would see to it that we took no part in any foreign war. Realists felt that the war issue which confronted the voters was not whether we would be at war in the next four years, but rather which candidate, which party, was best equipped to carry us to victory in the shooting war which they did not want but firmly expected nevertheless.

The home front issue was much clearer, and possibly exceeded the war front in determining votes. It was whether the social and economic changes born in the first eight Roosevelt years were to be carried on and extended by the men who had sired them, or carried on under a tighter rein by men who had originally opposed each and every one.

The campaign was most unusual in nearly all of its outward manifestations. First, the rival candidates themselves were both men of obvious stature and personal magnetism, which doesn't happen often. Second, there was political history-making in the very fact of their candidacies. Roosevelt was the first and—unless the Constitution is reamended someday—the last President to be given the nomination for a third term in the White House. Willkie was the first man who was a lifetime member of one major party and was nominated for President by the other.

It was also the first campaign in which federal laws supposedly limited the amount of money that could be spent for a candidate and the amount any individual could contribute. The restriction worked in reverse. It brought from both parties a pattern of evasion, plus record-breaking expenditures and individual contributions. From 1940 on, no one ever knew how much money had been poured out in a presidential campaign for either the winner or the loser.

And for the first time since the very earliest days of the Republic, foreign ideologies figured in a presidential campaign. Both American Communists who took their orders from Stalin and American Fascists who thought Hitlerism was a desirable import were active participants. Both sought the defeat of Roosevelt. Stalin and Hitler were temporary allies abroad, and there was American reaction to the brutally pragmatic alliance that had resulted in the overrunning of Poland and the partitioning of most of the rest of Europe into Fascist or Communist spheres of influence.

Finally, the campaign featured America's first peacetime conscription of the nation's manpower into the armed forces for a war both parties were pledged to avert.

The dramatic registration of sixteen million American men between the ages of twenty-one and thirty-six, in the same polling places where three weeks later fifty million voters were to cast their presidential ballots, was taken out of the field of partisan controversy by the two nominees—both holding it vital to the national defense. But no one could eliminate its affect on the national thinking. On both draft day and election day, particularly in the big cities, the lines outside the registry booths were long, and there were hours of waiting. People who took a look at the lines went back home for portable camp chairs or soap boxes. The sense of urgency, of national commitment, was everywhere.

These were the ways the 1940 campaign was different from others. Now for the similarities. The most obvious element of consistency in campaigns is that of timing. Come war or peace, prosperity or depression, hell or high water, they must be held in the scheduled fourth year. No administration can pick or choose as a British cabinet most often can, the time to submit its record to the electorate for endorsement. Congress has the power, under the Constitution, to change the day of the year, but otherwise there is no way of extending the tenure of the administration in power without an election.

There is a much more important sameness about presidential campaigns, also connected with timing, though not as obvious. The voter, and sometimes even the politician, talks and thinks of the presidential campaign starting in midsummer of the presidential year, when the candidates of the major parties have been selected. To him the campaign is made up of the rallies, parades, TV and radio oratory, the blare of sound-truck horns, all through September and October into the first week of November.

That is a misconception, consistent and recurring. The real presidential campaign starts in the summer of the *previous* year and comes to an end not on Election Day but in June or July, when the parties have finished the business of picking their nominees. That preconvention period is the time when the winning coalition comes into being and nothing of the oratory thereafter changes the result.

Writing in *Politics in the Empire State* * in 1947, I said:

> The factors that lead up to the nomination of the rival candidates—their personal ties and past records; their social views and the political economic and social forces lined up against them; the methods by which they are nominated, including the factor of party unity or discord—pretty well settle the election before a single speech is made by the candidates . . . After that, all is noise and confusion.

This appraisal implicitly rejects the supposed shifts in public sentiment recorded by the public opinion polls during the campaign, stemming from developments therein. It holds that the mind of the voter is made up in advance, whether or not he recognizes and admits that fact even to himself, and that all that happens in the course of the electioneering is a clearer identification of the factors that led to the nomination of the

* Warren Moscow, *Politics in the Empire State* (New York, Alfred A. Knopf, Inc., 1948), p. 236.

rival candidates in the first place. As the electioneering proceeds the voter finds justification, in the act of one candidate or the omission by the other, for the vote he always wanted to cast.

Even the Truman-Dewey election of 1948 was no exception. Truman talked issues at every whistle stop, Dewey conducted himself as though he were already President, and politics beneath him. This was enough to confirm the latent distaste for Dewey and the liking for Truman. Also, the refusal of the Republican 80th Congress to appropriate money for storage bins in which the farmer could store his surpluses had cost the GOP a large segment of the farm vote before the party conventions were even held.

The electoral votes of Illinois, Wisconsin and Ohio, all with substantial farm belts, as well as Missouri, Iowa and Minnesota, totaling 101, were out of the Dewey column where everyone expected them to be and on the Truman side instead.

The predestination which has been selected for each election started, as far as the 1940 campaign was concerned, two full years in advance. It was the result of a series of crises abroad, which occurred during that period with the regularity of the equinoxes. For those who need a reminder, here is the timetable of the things that were:

Spring, 1938—Hitler, after fomenting internal strife in Austria, marches in his army to restore order and forcibly annexes it to the German Reich.

Autumn, 1938—After similar preliminaries in Czechoslovakia, and threatening a general European war, Hitler wins the assent, at the Munich conference, of England and France to the dismemberment of Czechoslovakia, a democratic ally of England and France, on his own pledge that he will seek no additional territory in Europe. The agreement, hailed as bringing "peace in our time," stalled for exactly one year the start of World War II.

Spring, 1939—Hitler invades the remainder of a defenseless Czechoslovakia and sets his sights on Poland. England and France make it clear that if he attacks Poland, they will declare war.

Autumn, 1939—Hitler, to avoid a two-front war, makes a treaty with Stalin so that when he invades Poland, Russia, instead of fighting in Poland's behalf as France's ally, moves in as a co-aggressor. England and France declare war on Germany as Poland falls, but no real fighting occurs on land. What follows is a six-month period known in America as the "phony war," or *sitzkrieg,* with only sporadic sea or air raids and a small, separate war waged by Russia against little Finland.

Spring, 1940—A series of lightning strokes by Hitler's army, tanks and dive bombers brings him the domination of Western Europe. First he overruns Denmark and Norway, defeating a British counterinvasion of the latter; then he rolls his troops through neutral Holland and Belgium with a *blitzkrieg* that routs the British and conquers the French. The British achieve the "miracle of Dunkirk," evacuating their army almost intact, but without guns or equipment, and England stands alone in opposition to Hitler's forces.

Each and every one of the developments had its effect on American public opinion, which sometimes approved of developments, sometimes reacted against. At the time of Munich, when it was hoped that World War II had been averted by the sacrificing of the independent existence of Czechoslovakia, American sentiment was heavily for staying out of Europe's troubles, war or no war. When Poland was invaded, America reacted favorably, in general, to the decision of the British and French to fight Hitler's newest act of aggression.

Then came the period of the "phony war," or *sitzkrieg* as opposed to *blitzkrieg*. For more than six months after Poland fell to German dive bombers, tanks and mechanized infantry divisions, the German legions sat quietly behind the west wall Hitler had built along the Rhine, and the opposing British and French armies bivouacked behind France's Maginot Line. Nothing that looked like war went on, except for an occasional sea or air raid, and all attention went to Russia's attack on Finland, designed by the Russians to give them more of a territorial cushion in the northwest.

The virtual truce between the expected major opponents puzzled America, and gave support to those who thought the best America could do, then or at any other time, was to mind her own business and stay away from Europe's recurring problems.

From the beginning of the series of European crises, America's military weakness, in the form of an air force, an army and even a navy, had been obvious, and the President and Congress moved step by step along the long and expensive road to preparedness in case we became involved. The ability to sell new war equipment to England and France was an important part of our "tooling up" of military production, for we did not have the manpower in our armed forces to use the matériel we were preparing to produce.

In the middle 1930's, during Roosevelt's own first term, the Congress had passed and the President signed so-called neutrality legislation forbidding the sale of munitions to either side in any war. The impetus was the Nye armaments investigation, which produced evidence to back the premise that our role as a supplier of munitions in World War I had involved us in a war we would not otherwise have joined.

In September, 1939, on the heels of the Polish invasion and the start of World War II, we took the first step in discarding our role as a neutral. Roosevelt urged, and got through Congress, amendments to the 1935 law which permitted belligerents to buy arms and matériel in this country, provided they paid in cash and carried it home in their own ships.

The offer was open, theoretically, as much to Hitler as to his opponents, but in fact it favored—intentionally—England and France who controlled the surface of the seas. When opposition was expressed on the theory that it was the beginning of a new involvement, Roosevelt and the party platform of 1940 as well were disingenuous enough to present the neutrality amendments as ones that guaranteed our *non*involvement, since we gave up the right to sail our own ships with military cargoes any place we pleased.

If Hitlerism sank to a new low in the winter of 1939–40 in the collective mind of America, so did Russian Communism. Those who already hated or distrusted Communism were joined by many who had previously had illusions about, or even sympathies with, that so-called workers' movement. First came Stalin's cynical alliance with Hitler and Naziism in the division of Poland—and other spoils—in Eastern Europe. Second came the invasion of little Finland by Russia. America cheered every Russian stumble in that adventure. The mental picture grew of the world situation as democracies against the dictatorships. However, the sense of urgency, of our really being involved willy-nilly, was lacking.

That came in May and June of 1940, with the fall of Denmark, Norway, Belgium, Holland and France in rapid and terrifying progression. It seemed to many here that when England also toppled, as surely it must, we could be without the protection of the British fleet to police the Atlantic Ocean barrier, and that we would be the next major target.

All this as the preconvention political campaigns of both parties were heading toward their climaxes. There was no real argument in America against our bending all our efforts to build immediately—if not sooner—a two-ocean Navy to maintain the watch in the Pacific while defending us in the Atlantic.

There was violent and prolonged controversy over every other aspect. There were the very noisy American Nazis and Communists—open or disguised—who in the interest of their separate isms argued against any and every step by us aimed at impeding dictator-domination of Europe. There was a much more reputable and substantial group of people and public figures who felt that with England bound to collapse, and the dictators bound to triumph in Europe, we should do nothing more to antagonize the victors. We should build up our own defenses, accept the loss of Europe to the world of democracy, and hope for peaceful coexistence. Ex-President Herbert Hoover and aviation hero Charles A. Lindbergh emerged separately as the leading protagonists of that viewpoint.

Then there were the interventionists with varying strategies. Some felt we should continue to prop up England as long as there was an England, while we used the time we were able to buy in postponing her downfall to build up our own defenses. There were others who would go further—scrap even technical neutrality if necessary to prevent the dictators, particularly Hitler, from achieving final victory. The principal member of this latter group—and he would have been of tremendous importance even had he stood all alone—was the President of the United States, Franklin D. Roosevelt. But not even he talked of our armed intervention.

The "miracle of Dunkirk" came in June, when the nation would otherwise have had its eyes centered on the domestic American miracles, the national conventions of the political parties. Roosevelt then took the step which robbed America of its last pretense of official neutrality. A British Army that had lost even its rifles while clambering aboard small craft to escape from France was rearmed by us with a million rifles and thousands of machine guns—equipment we had had in storage since World War I—so that it could defend the home island if Hitler followed his victory in France with an invasion of Britain.

Roosevelt moved without even submitting the matter to Congress or broadcasting his intentions in advance. But the refusal of the British to quit in the face of odds that looked overwhelming; Churchill's great speech pledging a fight on the beaches, the landing fields, the streets and the hills; his pledge that the British Navy would be based if necessary in the New World to carry on the war; all thrilled America to the point that our contribution—arming her for a last stand—won applause rather than criticism from the vast majority of Americans who did not want us in the war, but also wanted Hitler to lose.

Thus far we have had the broad outlines of the setting of the nomination of candidates for the Presidency in 1940. Much has been written about both of them since. It is worthwhile taking a look at them as they were at the time.

Franklin D. Roosevelt and Wendell Willkie had much in common. Both were big men physically—handsome extroverts who loved to talk and laugh and be with people. Each had the personal confidence born of demonstrated success; each naturally dominated any room in which he was. They were men with quick minds, great readers who remembered what they had read. Both had traveled extensively in America and knew the people, the problems of each section. They were ten years apart in age, Roosevelt fifty-eight and Willkie forty-eight. Politically they both possessed that intangible appeal to a following as important to candidates as sex appeal to any would-be Romeo. There was one great difference—Roosevelt was, in politics and government, the brilliant, experienced professional, Willkie an aspiring amateur.

This difference shows up most vividly in a timetable of their careers:

Roosevelt 1882—Born in Dutchess County, New York.
1910—Elected to a two-year term in the New York State Senate, upper house of the Legislature.
1912—Re-elected.
1913—Moves to Washington as Assistant Secretary of the Navy in the cabinet of President Woodrow Wilson, serving until 1920.
1914—Runs unsuccessfully for United States Senator from New York in the first pri-

mary held under the new system of direct election of senators.

1920—Is nominated by the Democratic National Convention for Vice-President of the United States, on the ticket headed by James M. Cox of Ohio for President, and goes down to defeat, with Cox, in the Republican "Harding landslide" of that year.

1921—Is stricken by poliomyelitis, leaving him deprived of normal use of his legs for the rest of his life.

1924—Wins national applause for his speech, delivered while standing with crutches, nominating the liberal Alfred E. Smith for President, in which he hailed Smith as the "Happy Warrior."

1928—Is elected Governor of New York by the narrow margin of 28,000 votes.

1930—Is re-elected Governor by the record-breaking majority of 725,000.

1932—Is elected President of the United States, getting a popular vote of 22,821,857 against 15,761,841 for the incumbent President Herbert Hoover, with an electoral majority of 472 to 59.

1936—Is re-elected President, with a popular vote of 27,751,597 to 16,679,583 for the Republican, Governor Alf M. Landon of Kansas, and an all-time high electoral majority of 523 to 8.

1940—Becomes the first President in American history to be nominated for a third term in office.

Willkie 1892—Born in Elwood, Indiana.

1915—Begins practice of law as a member of family law firm headed by his father and mother.

1917—Enlists as a private in the U.S. Army at

the start of World War I, and remains in for the duration.

1919—Declines offer of the Democratic nomination for Congress from his home district in Indiana.

1919—Moves to Akron, Ohio, to further his career at the bar. Works briefly as a staff attorney for the Firestone Rubber Company, and for the balance of a decade as counsel for the local electric company. Is active in American Legion and other communal affairs.

1924—Attends Democratic National Convention of that year as a district delegate from Ohio, reflecting his standing in the community rather than activity in politics.

1929—Moves to New York to become counsel to the newly formed Commonwealth & Southern public utility holding company.

1932—Becomes President of Commonwealth & Southern. Attends 1932 Democratic National Convention as a worker for Newton D. Baker, choice that year of many big businessmen for the Democratic nomination.

1935—Is selected a Democratic County Committee member by Tammany Hall from the East Side "silk stocking" district.

1935—Becomes spokesman for the American public utilities in their fight with the Roosevelt Administration, first against government entry into the competitive power business, via the TVA and later against the regulatory decree which outlawed public utility holding companies by June of 1940.

1938–39—Becomes a frequent spokesman and author of speeches and articles attacking the encroachment of government in areas

previously dominated by private industry.
1940—Is nominated for President of the United States on the Republican ticket.

Both were blessed with courage and a disdain for convention. And both were lucky. Roosevelt used to talk casually of his own "lucky star."

When Franklin Roosevelt entered politics in 1910, his fifth cousin, ex-President Theodore Roosevelt, was still the most dynamic force on the American political scene. The Roosevelt name was thus a valuable asset, and it helped young Franklin, when he decided on government as a career, to get the Democratic nomination for State Senator from the Hudson River Valley district in which his family had long been residents and landowners. The Dutchess County Roosevelts stemmed from the same seventeenth-century Dutch settler as did Theodore, but their branch had intermarried with the seafaring British-stock Delanos who made their fortune in the China trade. For no particular reason, the Hudson River Roosevelts were Democrats. It was a wealthy family in which Franklin was the only child in his branch, so that had he been so disposed, he would have spent his life working no harder than supervising the family estate. Instead he used this background of financial security to bolster the uncertainties of political office-holding.

Franklin could never have been elected from his traditionally Republican home district if Theodore had not been engaged, at the same time, in splitting the Republican Party nationwide into two irreconcilable wings, his own followers against those of William Howard Taft, the President he had picked as his own successor. The fight was waged in individual states in 1910, and nationwide in 1912. It served, by dividing the Republican votes, to elect Roosevelt to the New York legislature in 1910 and to re-elect him in 1912, just as it put Woodrow Wilson into the White House that year as a minority President.

In his first few weeks in Albany, Roosevelt showed he had no intention of remaining in the background, of being just a political accident. In that era, United States senators were still chosen by state legislatures. In Albany the Democrats had a majority that took its political orders from Charles F. Murphy, leader of Tammany Hall, then as later a national symbol of the political corrupt machine.

When Murphy ordered the election of a hack to the U.S. Senate, Roosevelt organized a bloc of legislative liberals who bolted the Democratic caucus and deadlocked the legislature for many weeks before Murphy came up with a compromise selection. Roosevelt's daring gave him national headlines he could have won in no other way, and established him as an independent, anti-Tammany Democrat.

It might still have been only a short-lived victory—for openly opposing Murphy was then hardly the path for promotion in New York politics—except that in 1912 Murphy backed Champ Clark against Woodrow Wilson for the presidential nomination, and Wilson won. The promotion of young Roosevelt, established as an anti-Tammany man, to a post in Washington was a natural gesture for the incoming President.

When FDR thus went to Washington as Assistant Secretary of the Navy—a position once held by Theodore—no one had any idea that World War I was on its way and that America's first and possibly most important contribution to the eventual Allied victory would be made by the Navy, guarding the lifeline of supplies and later troops to an embattled Europe.

Roosevelt emerged after eight years in the Navy Department with great credit, though tabbed by some as overly ambitious for one who was only second in command. He had tried to get out in 1914—before the war loomed as important to us—by running in the newly established primary for the United States Senatorship from New York. He lost in the primary, fortunately, because 1914 was a bad year in New York for the Democrats, and he or any other Democrat would have lost the general election. So he was not too scarred as a loser.

In 1920, when James M. Cox of Ohio emerged from a protracted Democratic National Convention as the nominee for President, he selected Roosevelt as his running mate and got the convention to agree. Murphy, still running New York, gruffly assented to this surprising selection because he appreciated Cox's act of clearing the nomination first with the home state boss. Cox wanted Roosevelt because he was young and attractive, had made a good war record in the Navy Department, bore the name Roosevelt, which was still good for votes, and balanced the ticket by bringing in a New Yorker who was also a non-Tammany New Yorker.

The Cox-Roosevelt ticket went down to overwhelming defeat in the landslide of 1920, reflecting America's desire to change control in Washington, forget the war, and get back to "normalcy," a word invented by GOP candidate Harding. But the experience of running for national office was invaluable to loser Roosevelt. He had had presidential ambitions, now they were sharpened. He toured the country as no other vice-presidential nominee had ever done, with his own campaign train and entourage, making speeches and friends everywhere, getting personal knowledge of the different sections of the country—who was who and why in almost every state of the Union.

When polio laid Roosevelt low, although he was flat on his back he never gave up the dream of the Presidency. His wealthy, doting mother wanted him to take it easy and retire from the world. Instead he wrote letters across the country, keeping up on political and governmental affairs, associating himself with issues, keeping people aware of his existence. His 1924 speech for Smith at Madison Square Garden, his first major public appearance, was a howling success—if not for Smith who failed to get the nomination that year. Roosevelt was reminding politicians of his continued identity as a fighting Democratic liberal.

His biggest break came in 1928 when Smith, Governor of New York, was nominated for President. Smith, the first Catholic nominee of a major party, felt he needed Roosevelt, a prominent Protestant, heading the ticket in New York as the candidate for Governor to help him carry his pivotal home state.

Roosevelt at first refused to run. He felt that he could use four more years at Georgia's Warm Springs, which he had developed as a recovery center for polio victims, to recover the use of his own legs. Moreover, there was a matter of political timing involved. If he ran for Governor of New York in 1928 and was re-elected in 1930, that would make him a natural candidate for President in 1932. But Roosevelt felt that 1928 was a Republican year; that Hoover would win and would be re-elected in 1932. This timetable called for Roosevelt to run for Governor of New York no sooner than 1932, and President in 1936. His political luck ordained that Smith would refuse to take no for an answer in 1928 and that Hoover's tenure in the Presidency was terminated by an economic depression that no one then envisaged.

Roosevelt was lucky also in that during the Depression years of 1930, 1931 and 1932, Hoover showed up as a prime believer in the theory that government should stay out of people's lives even if they were hungry, while Roosevelt, occupying the principal state house in the nation, showed up appositely as a governmental activist who with the agencies of his state government tried to aid those who needed help. Hoover occupied the White House and Roosevelt the Governor's Mansion in a period when the White House showed up to poor advantage.

There is no need here to review each and every facet of the New Deal that Roosevelt brought to Washington in his first term as President and continued, even more controversially, in his second. Suffice it to say that his eight years were the most exciting of any President since Andrew Jackson a bit more than a century earlier. He aroused much the same loyalties and hatreds and party positioning as the Jackson regime. In 1940, when he proposed to extend his own tenure, emotions, for and against, reached their peak in intensity.

Now for his opponent. Willkie came from a family of small-town intellectuals as ruggedly individualistic as any branch of the Roosevelt tribe, and Wendell, while very much of a hail-fellow-well-met in his public encounters, was very much like his forebears in his private life and thoughts. The Willkie ancestors went back only two generations in this country, having come from Germany in the middle 1800's when so many gave up on the Old World and sought life and more freedom in the New.

The Willkie ancestors settled in Indiana, then principally a farm state dotted with villages and small towns. His father Herman was superintendent of schools in Elwood when he met and married Henrietta Trisch, schoolteacher. Herman Willkie gave up his post in the school system to practice law. Henrietta studied law, and the Indiana records indicate she was the first woman admitted to the bar in that state. Herman Willkie acted as counsel to Elwood's striking tin workers at a time when a labor strike was regarded as a foul blow at the American free enterprise system. Henrietta was unique in that she went to work instead of staying home and keeping house.

They had five sons, of whom Wendell was the fourth, and a daughter, all brought up by their parents to think for themselves and do for themselves. Wendell, as a teen-ager, worked in the summer, first at the local tin plate works, later on as a migrant worker pitching hay on a farm, or driving a bus at Yellowstone Park. He went to law school and worked in the family law firm briefly before going off to World War I. When he returned, his mother insisted that he strike out on his own, and she had her way by declining to admit him to the family law practice again. He moved himself and his bride to Akron, Ohio, never to return to Indiana for more than visits and vacations.

His first job, with the Firestone Rubber Company, involved no real practice of the law, just the giving of legal advice to Firestone employees as part of an early better employee relationship program Harvey Firestone had instituted. To Wendell, who had been a college orator and campus activist, this was dull stuff, and he soon quit to enter a small Akron law firm as a partner. Not long after, he was specializing as the trial counsel defending the local public utility company in lawsuits brought against it. It was an art in which he shone, with his quick mind, ready wit and good legal background. And he attracted the attention of Bernard Capen Cobb, the head of a utility chain of which Willkie's company, the Northern Ohio Power and Light, was a subsidiary. Cobb happened to be one of the few entrepreneurs of the utility business in the 1920's who did not make a practice of gypping both the customers and stockholders.

This was a major stroke of luck for Willkie. His work in the courts was independent of company rate or investment policies, and he could have carried on with equal ability and good grace if the Northern Ohio had happened to be part of a chain dominated by Samuel Insull or Howard Hopson. But if that had been so, he would have been stained later when the Insull and Hopson empires crashed scandalously. He would never have emerged, as he did, as the respectable spokesman for the respectable elements in the power business.

But Cobb marked Willkie as a coming young man, and when the Cobb interests were formally united in the Commonwealth & Southern holding company in the spring of 1929, he persuaded Willkie to give up Akron, its small city comforts and conveniences, and move to New York as counsel to the Commonwealth & Southern. Cobb had in mind the grooming of Willkie to succeed himself as C & S president whenever he retired. This he did in 1932. So Willkie was elected president of the big utility combine the same year that Franklin D. Roosevelt was elected President of the United States.

Franklin D. Roosevelt ran four times, against different opponents, for the Presidency of the United States, defeating them all. Of the four, Willkie was the only one he both liked and respected.

2 The Background: The Republicans

The Republican Party took such a series of beatings at the polls in the presidential and congressional elections between 1928 and 1938 that it lost a bit more faith in itself each additional time the votes were counted and it was at the short end. In one election or another, its best "name" candidates went down to defeat and its long-established political and financial leadership either quit or was hopelessly ensconced in the public's doghouse.

The 1928 election of Hoover had affirmed the GOP's position as the unquestioned majority party in the nation, the symbol of prosperity, respectability and power. Then "everything went black." The first effect of the stock market crash of 1929 was to strip the Republicans, at the 1930 election, of working control of Congress, though the party retained nominal majorities. Two additional years which saw the nation bogged down in hopeless depression cost the party the Presidency and the Congress. Franklin D. Roosevelt took over the White House and in short order was boss of the Congress, the nation and all its financial and economic activities.

Though the nation's economy staged a noticeable recovery in the following two years, the Republican condition grew worse. Not only did the nation approve of Roosevelt's program of action and more action, but everything the Republicans prized as valuable or sacred was kicked around in the mud of congressional investigations.

The sacred cows of Wall Street, leaders of business and high finance, were exposed in all their stupidity and venality; the great public utility empires were shown up as stock-jobbing and pocket-lining devices of their creators. As the nation cheered, the Republicans groaned.

Nearly all those caught with their hands in the nation's economic till were Republicans. For decades Wall Street and the public utilities had run the Republican Party, and through it the nation, with the controls in the velvet glove of the House of Morgan. The Democrats rode so high, and the Republicans sank so low, that in 1934—for the first time in the history of the two-party system—the *ins* won additional seats at the interim congressional election.

Then things seemed to take a turn for the better. Roosevelt's hit or miss attacks on the Depression began producing enough visible errors to give the GOP hopes for 1936. Professional politicians know that a party's fortunes at the polls can zoom even faster than they can sink; that there is usually nothing wrong with a major party that getting back into power can't cure. The bitterest intraparty differences have been resolved by what has been so cynically described as "the cohesive power of public plunder."

The prize example of the quick comeback involved the Democrats. They had reached their nadir in the defeat of Al Smith by Hoover. Their deep regional and religious differences seemed to bode them no future as a party; there was nothing to keep them together. There had even been serious suggestions that the Democratic Party change its name to get away from its past. Yet opposition mistakes, economic disaster and the side issue of Prohibition's repeal had brought the donkey braying back into the White House only four years thereafter, fresher and more vigorous than ever.

So the Republicans developed hopes for 1936—the most

widespread hopes, and the falsest in electoral college history. For the experienced Republican politicians and the nation's big businessmen, by this time almost unanimously anti-New Deal, parlayed their wish-hope combinations into delusions of grandeur in the ten months of 1936 that preceded Election Day.

In the light of the result—Roosevelt won over Alf M. Landon of Kansas by an electoral vote of 523 to 8 and a popular vote of 27,751,597 to 16,679,583—the Republican optimism during the campaign seemed largely based on insanity.

The GOP leaders were generals, colonels and captains of an army who didn't realize their enlisted men had deserted. They were the "upper crust," used to running an America that they just *knew* was fundamentally too sound to re-elect that wild man Roosevelt; that given a chance would send packing all the college professors, social workers, radicals and Communists in Washington who were making a mockery of the American system. As devotees of the balanced budget, they couldn't see the voters approving an administration that was on a spending spree of $8 billion a year in its budget, and had run the national debt up from $27 billion to $40 billion. They assumed that conservative Democrats who bolted the New Deal between 1934 and 1936—like former presidential nominees John W. Davis and Al Smith, other bigwigs like John J. Raskob, Bainbridge Colby and James A. Reed—represented widespread defection in the opposition ranks.

They disapproved bitterly of the "lunatic fringe" which they claimed was running the country, but nevertheless counted heavily on help from its least responsible edges. They quietly helped finance a ragtag and bobtail outfit which under the name of the Union Party nominated for President a farmer-Congressman from North Dakota, William Lemke. Lemke was best known for House sponsorship of a farm subsidy plan the GOP violently opposed. The Union Party ticket was spearheaded by three men, none of them Lemke.

One was Father Charles E. Coughlin, an ambitious radio

priest who had a tremendous following on the airwaves. The second was Dr. Francis E. Townsend, with a quick-money plan for the elderly and millions of Townsend Club members who saw hope in it. The third was Gerald L. K. Smith, fresh from the late Huey Long's operations in Louisiana. He was a professional rabble-rouser in search of rabble.

Earlier in the year Republican fat cats had contributed at least $100,000 to push Herman Talmadge, a be-gallused Governor of Georgia, as an independent candidate of the George Wallace persuasion. When the Talmadge move got nowhere, they slipped additional money to the Smith, Townsend, Coughlin group, on the theory that this curious collection of left, right and wrong would draw millions of votes from Roosevelt. It made, as might be supposed, a large amount of noise when organized, but at the polls drew one of the smallest third-party totals of record. Their Union Party was the first modern manifestation of what was later called "the radical right," though the resemblance appeared later.

What really put the GOP on cloud nine for the duration of the 1936 campaign was the *Literary Digest* poll, the best known of its day. It had a proper claim to infallibility. When the *Literary Digest*, a news magazine, took its first presidential straw vote in 1924, it hit the electoral college vote exactly on the digits. It did almost as well in 1928 and 1932, and in the widely advertised New York City mayoralty election of 1933 which put La Guardia into City Hall. It never had picked a loser.

Its straw vote aimed at a large and random rather than select segment of the electorate. In 1936 it sent out its usual 10,000,000 postcards, got back its normal percentage return of 2,500,000, and on the basis of the vote count flatly predicted Landon's election. It said he would carry thirty-two of the forty-eight states, with 56 per cent of the popular vote. The flop, which helped put the *Digest* out of business, has usually been blamed on its mailing lists, culled from the telephone directories and motor vehicle lists, and therefore unrepresentative in 1936 of the lower income solidarity for Roosevelt. But that was only partly the reason.

The undisputed boss of the *Literary Digest* was an elderly gentleman who moved in the best business and social circles and had never met anyone who wasn't for Landon. Like most of the Republican high command, he interviewed himself and his best friends and came away convinced. To him any poll that failed to register the overwhelming anti-Roosevelt sentiment was all wrong. Underlings resolved the dilemma he created for them by stacking the straws. They sent out twice as many postcards to traditional Republican territory as to Democratic areas in order to produce the result their publisher demanded. Newspapermen who had access to the regional breakdowns given out with the totals spotted the tactic early in the game and marked the poll as an unreliable indicator of the election ahead.

But those who wanted to believe believed, even experienced professionals in the Republican Party. Every one of the six division heads named by Republican National Chairman John D. M. Hamilton to help run the Landon campaign sent Hamilton a private, confidential prediction of a Landon sweep. Hamilton made a public prediction based on those reports, but privately counted only Maine, Vermont, Kansas, Nebraska and South Dakota in the Landon column. He wasn't much further away than Jim Farley, his Democratic opposite number. Farley won a place in the history books for his public forecast of Maine and Vermont for Landon, and all the rest for Roosevelt. Afterwards, Farley told reporters he would have conceded New Hampshire as well had it not been for the particularly vehement protests of the Democratic chairman there.

The debacle brought the Republican Party to a new low. In the Senate, where men run only every six years, the veterans who had squeaked through in 1930 this time lost out in the landslide. The Republicans were down to a handful of Governors and in either House of Congress had fewer than 20 per cent of the membership. And the old political leadership, discredited or discouraged by defeat, chose this time to step aside.

For many years the party's most influential and representative leader had been Charles D. Hilles of New York. Courtly, personable and conservative, he was the man who sat down with the bankers and financiers and translated their thinking into appropriate Republican policy. He had been chairman of the Republican National Committee during William Howard Taft's Presidency; had sat in the smoke-filled room of Chicago's Hotel Blackstone and helped pick Warren G. Harding as the nation's next President after Woodrow Wilson. His connections were not only with high finance, but with the Republican Party of the Southern states, which lived on a diet of federal postmasterships and "expense" money given the delegations they sent to Republican National Conventions.

Hilles, who had neither favored nor fought the Landon nomination, announced after the 1936 disaster that he was stepping off the national committee he had so greatly influenced since 1912. It marked the end of the direct, systematized Wall Street control, as Hilles allies stepped down or out then or shortly after. J. Henry Roraback, undisputed boss of Connecticut and most of New England, was seriously ill in 1936 and committed suicide in 1937. His tie-in was with the public utilities. New England's rapid flowing rivers and numerous waterwheels had made the region manufacturing and power-conscious even before the day of electricity, and Roraback's tactics and personality kept it that way.

In New Jersey, banker Daniel E. Pomeroy, another Hilles ally, stayed on as national committeeman, but was diminished in stature without Hilles' support. In Pennsylvania, where first Boies Penrose and then William S. Vare had run the nation's most powerful and corrupt machine in close alliance with the Pennsylvania Manufacturers Association, the state had gone Democratic for the first time since the Civil War. Vare was dead. So was his machine. Into the vacuum slowly moved multimillionaire Joseph N. Pew of the Sun Oil Company.

Pew was part of a new breed of Republican leaders who came into being with the withdrawal of the old. Generally they operated as individuals, relying on their own judgment and their own money power. They usually were lacking in subtlety and experience, and to each his own status usually came first. Another was Colonel Robert R. McCormick, owner of the *Chicago Tribune*. He used it as his personal organ to run the city of Chicago and the state of Illinois and even to influence Republican politicians in Indiana and Wisconsin, where the *Tribune* also circulated. He would have liked to run the Republican Party in the nation.

But basically Pew and McCormick and their kind, even the more realistic crew which focused itself behind Thomas E. Dewey in New York after 1937, had only local prestige and a localized circle of friends. Gone was the pervasive national relationship with the House of Morgan. Wall Street had lost not only control of its own destinies, but of the local banks and businesses which in turn had influence on local politicians. The public utility network still existed but its members were not disposed to throw their weight around. They were concerned with survival. For the first time in its history the Republican Party lacked a national alliance of top bosses who, teamed together, could exercise the appropriate pressures on the party structure—force the appropriate nomination or resist the unconventional.

The midterm congressional election of 1938 brought it eighty-one additional Republican seats in the House as well as eight in the slower-to-turn-over Senate, the greatest comeback in numbers in midterm election history. It also brought new hopes, new faces. In New York, Tom Dewey's close run for Governor against the redoubtable Herbert Lehman made the young racket-buster a man of national note for reasons other than the gunmen he had sent to jail. Ohio, traditional "mother of Presidents," had reared this time two sons of seeming stature.

One was John W. Bricker, elected Governor, and the second was Robert A. Taft, fifty-year-old son of the former President, who defeated a leading New Dealer for election to the U.S. Senate. Connecticut elected as Governor its first Democrat since 1930, Raymond Baldwin. Pennsylvania reverted to the Republican column by putting Arthur James in its Harrisburg State House.

Good as they looked to their supporters, the realists knew that each had handicaps in a role of presidential aspirant. Dewey was still only District Attorney of New York County and would be thirty-eight years old when the presidential election was held. Taft was still a first-term senator. Bricker, who looked like a President—someone called him "an honest Harding"—was handicapped by being unable to contest Ohio's delegation with Taft. Arthur Vandenberg of Michigan, who might have posed for a picture of the composite senator, had no great appeal.

Of dark horses there were many—Senator Styles Bridges of New Hampshire, House Minority Leader Joseph W. Martin of Massachusetts, Minority Leader of the Senate Charles McNary of Oregon, former American Legion Commander Hanford MacNider of Iowa, the newly elected Governor James in Pennsylvania—but to the Republican rank and file they all looked like possible vice-presidential choices at best.

The most attractive man around was young Harold Stassen of Minnesota, but by 1940 Stassen would be only thirty-three, not old enough to hold the presidential office. As a result, he had many friends, and no enemies.

The most established, experienced contender was Herbert Hoover, hovering in the background, ready and willing to seek the Presidency again. Hoover knew it would be beneath his dignity to openly go out after delegates, but the hope of being nominated, running for vindication, never left his mind. He went to the Republican convention of 1936 as the principal invited speaker.

He delivered a carefully prepared hell-raising speech aimed at stampeding the convention in his direction. He got rousing applause, but no support as a candidate. He was to do the same thing, under the same circumstances, at the 1940 convention, with the same result. The delegates did not want to go into a campaign, either in 1936 or in 1940, with "Hooverism" as the issue. Deservedly or not, he was still the symbol of the Depression.

Either as candidate or orator, Hoover regarded every act of the New Deal as a personal insult, a calculated reflection on his own Administration. But the Republican Party as a whole did not dare pledge itself to unqualified repeal of the New Deal, the ending of its reforms and benefits. Many would have accepted Hoover's philosophy, even if not Hoover. The vast majority of the Republican leaders and campaign contributors regarded the New Deal controls of the nation's economy as an obnoxious invasion of their own rights as Americans; they resented the growth and tactics of labor unions protected for the first time by government itself; they privately viewed government handouts to the needy in the cities and to the farmers on the land as weakening the nation's moral fiber.

There was a much smaller group which felt that the Roosevelt era had brought some long-needed reforms, that there never should even if there ever could be a return to the good old days. The New Deal might be sloppily and politically administered, but it had given the stricken nation a badly needed dose of smelling salts. It should not be attacked in toto, but only for its mistakes and excesses.

This group won out in the form, if not the substance, of the party's public expression in the period preceding 1940 simply because its approach was the only politic one. At the climax of the 1936 campaign, the Republicans had lashed out at the new Social Security program about to go into effect. By arrangement, big employers stuffed the pre-election pay envelopes of their workers with literature warning them that they were about to take a pay cut to finance the system, and that its benefits were dubious. The move worried the Democrats for a few days, but the backfire effect was obvious in the election returns.

By 1939 no one was ready again to challenge the Social Security system, already paying out unemployment insurance as well as retirement benefits. Even those most irate over sit-down strikes demanded changes in the Wagner Labor Relations Act, not the end of labor-organizing rights. Much as they disliked tax monies going in cash payments to farmers for not raising crops, they had to pledge continuation of some kind of farm benefits, or their presidential nominee could kiss good-by to the farm states' vote.

They could lash out at the waste and looseness of administration in the WPA or the PWA, but not government's obligation to keep starvation from the door of millions of families, so they urged it would work better with local or state administration, with all the bums and grifters removed from the work relief rolls. There were New Deal inventions—like federal bank deposit insurance, federal home mortgage loans at low interest that could be paid off like rent, the Civilian Conservation Corps that combined conservation work with health-building jobs for the young unemployed—that the Republican orators did not attack at all.

Generally, the Republican posture on domestic issues was that the New Deal was wastefully administered by a party that didn't know how to govern, that it was punitive and divisive, and that the Republican Party, given the chance, could achieve whatever desirable objectives the New Deal professed in a way that was better, fairer and cheaper. This marked the birth of what was later to be assailed as the "me too" approach, and to be blamed for a whole succession of failures at the polls.

No one will ever know if the Republicans could have won in 1940 with their stand on domestic issues. Events in other parts of the world moved in on the American people, vying for first place in their thinking. From the Munich crisis of September, 1938, to Pearl Harbor on December 7, 1941, America was divided sharply and, ultimately, bitterly in its feelings about the country's proper role. In those debates, waged more often than not on grounds that rose far above partisan politics, the

Republicans occupied a position which became less enviable as the pressures grew. Even the timetable operated against them. The prewar period served to harden the position of a majority of the Republican presidential hopefuls, and the party itself, against America's involvement in any way in another European war.

And then, in May, 1940, the "phony war" became a real war as Norway, Denmark, Belgium, Holland, Luxemburg and then France were overrun and conquered. A majority of the leading Republicans had already committed themselves to a definite policy of noninterference, noninvolvement, nonintervention, a position increasingly unpalatable as well as unrealistic.

There never was much dissent in America about the two other aggressor nations. Soviet Russia first shared with Nazi Germany in the partition by force of Poland, and then embarked on her own in an onslaught against little Finland. America's sentiments were rabidly anti-Communist. Finland had the best public relations with America of any nation in Europe, for it was the only one which year after year had paid the interest and principal installments on its World War I debt. To it we gave financial aid as a matter of course, and if it had been more accessible, we would have thought of sending military aid as well. Nor was there much doubt about how we felt about the other active aggressor, Japan. In the Far East it was carrying on a seven-year undeclared war against Chiang Kai-shek's China and casting obviously covetous eyes on all of the Occidental outposts in Asia from the Philippines to Singapore. America had been given years of magazine and newspaper exposure to the "yellow peril" of Japan, and everybody was "agin" it.

It was how to deal with Hitler that divided the American people as well as handicapped the Republicans.

Roosevelt was increasingly sympathetic to the democracies in his public declarations, reinforcing his feelings with aid, step by step, just as fast as he felt the people would follow. He brought into being the concept of "all aid short of war." He moved for repeal of the laws that prohibited Allied credit in this country until the World War I debts were paid; he started selling "surplus" American planes and arms, using the argument that a double American purpose was being served by delaying aggression and tooling up our own defense armament plants for replacement.

From the point of view of the Republican presidential possibilities, this buildup of alignment with the European democracies was sheer madness. That Man was going to drag us into a European war just as the last Democratic President had done. We had been in Europe in 1917 for the same reason, to save the world for democracy, and we had failed; this time we'd be better off staying out and minding our own business.

Men like Hoover and Bricker and Taft and Vandenberg firmly believed in and came out publicly for the concept of a "fortress America"; we were three thousand miles away, and if we built up our own defenses, we would be safe from attack. We should never again send our youth abroad to fight in a foreign war. Dewey's position was less definite but just as noninterventionist, sufficient to give him the support of the *Chicago Tribune*. While there were a number of outstanding Republicans who favored from the beginning all aid short of war—men like Henry L. Stimson of New York and William Allen White of Kansas—there were none in the ranks of the original presidential contenders.

The division in America was sectional to a great extent. The East, Republican as well as Democratic, was largely international minded. In key Eastern states the influence of the first and second generation of immigrants from Europe in favor of the democracies was a political factor to be reckoned with. The Jews were unanimous in their hatred of Hitler, as were the Poles, the Czechs and even those from Eastern Europe who feared rather than knew the worst for their homelands. There were enough voters of English, Scotch, French, Belgian and Scandinavian descent to be a formidable influence. Generally the peoples of the big cities along the Atlantic seacoast, who heard of the bombing of Warsaw, and later Rotterdam, London and Paris, feared for themselves if Hitler remained unchecked. Only some Irish, with their hatred of England, and some of the Germans infected by Naziism, took the "let's stay out of it" position.

The South, with an economy based on export, had been internationally minded throughout the history of the nation. People who could trace their lineage back to England and Scotland were the dominant majority. The South was as unhappy as any section over the prospect of war, but it was willing to take the risk.

Only the West and Far West were really safe territory for the isolationists. Europe seemed so far away, in days when domestic air travel was still a novelty, and the new transatlantic service consisted of lumbering flying boats which could not make the trip nonstop. The nation's farmers, proportionately greater in numbers and influence than later, thought more about the weather and crops than things beyond their view.

Thus, in terms of domestic politics, the international turmoil presented a greater electoral problem to the Republicans than to the Democrats. The Democrats, counting then on a solid South, could achieve an electoral majority by carrying the South and the industrial East, both interventionist minded. The Republicans needed, for their possible electoral majority, a combination of the isolationist strength west of the Alleghenies, plus the industrial and interventionist states of the Northeast.

Public reaction nationally, as measured by the monthly Gallup poll, was both curious and consistent. The Gallup interviewers reported that a majority of the people favored our staying out of the European conflict; felt that the democracies could not win without our help; that we should give them all aid short of war; and that this stand would involve us in the war eventually.

By the early spring of 1940 it was apparent that a number of the potential Republican candidates had been eliminated as possible winners of the election, though they and their followers would not concede. Taft, generally eschewing primaries, had quietly consolidated delegate strength among the Republican Old Guard and in the South, using political machinery that dated back to his father's time. But the argument that he could not win carried weight, just as it was to do a dozen years later when he came so close to being the nominee instead of Dwight Eisenhower.

Bricker dropped out because he could never get started. He and Taft, rather than fight for the Ohio delegation and break up one of the few smooth-running Republican machines in existence, made an unpublicized agreement that Bricker would withdraw and support Taft. If Taft failed in 1940, either at the nomination or election stage, Bricker was to have Ohio and Taft's support for 1944. Both sides lived up to their bargain.

Vandenberg supporters tried their man out in a few primaries, where he lost more delegates than he won. The only consistent primary winner was Dewey, who won some where he was opposed, and others unopposed. His major asset was the commanding lead he had over all his opposition, combined, in the monthly reports of the Gallup poll. Up to the appearance of Willkie as a contender, and the invasion of the Lowlands of Holland and Belgium by Hitler a few weeks thereafter, Dewey's ranking was that of the choice of 60 per cent of the Republicans.

Dewey toured the East, New England, the Midwest and the West, seeking delegate commitments comparable to his poll ratings. But the Republican state organizations, directed by no central leadership, were playing it coy, making as few commitments as possible in advance of the convention. In fact, by the time the whole thousand delegates had actually been selected at primaries or in convention or committee meetings, only 276 were actually pledged to any one of seven possibilities. Of these Dewey had 150, and many more promises of friendly consideration or first ballot support, if nothing happened to change the minds of the particular organizations involved.

It was explained to his managers and to him, time and time again, that the delegates preferred to go to the convention and look at the situation as it existed at nominating time. The party was in dead earnest in looking for the man who had the best chance to win, especially since it seemed inevitable that Franklin D. Roosevelt would again be the party's opponent.

Dewey slipped for the first time in the Gallup poll after the invasion of the Lowlands and the fall of France, and those who didn't like the cocky little New Yorker remarked gleefully that "Tom Dewey was the first American casualty" of World War II.

The situation was ripe for a new entry, if he looked like a winner, and the Willkie drive, long under way behind the scenes, began to really roll in full view of an increasingly interested and stimulated Republican Party membership at all levels.

3 The Background: The Democrats

The Democrats looked ahead to the 1940 campaign with more trepidation than confidence. Only once before had they held on to the White House for as many as eight consecutive years, and they were not accustomed to thinking in terms of a longer lease. They evinced constant concern over the possible effect at the polls of bickering and jealousies between the New Dealers and the party regulars.

Few realized that the coalition which gave the party its landslide victory in 1936 was enduring and would make the Democratic Party the majority party in the nation for decades ahead. Harry Hopkins, the social worker turned Presidential agent and operator, was quoted as having said "we will spend and spend, tax and tax, and elect and elect," but this attracted more attention as an indiscretion and controversy over whether he had actually said it than as a realistic forecast of things to come.

The 1936 coalition behind Franklin D. Roosevelt's second term candidacy was the closest thing to a European-style popular front that America had ever seen. It was new to both major parties. Starting after the Civil War, when the Democrats and Republicans became entrenched in a two-party system, the Democratic base had been the sectional vote of the

Solid South, not sufficient in itself for an electoral majority, but constant enough to give the Southerners seniority in Congress. A Southern Democrat had to worry only about his party primary, for the Republicans in the eleven states of the old Confederacy posed only token opposition, if any at all, on Election Day. The Democrats also had pockets of continuing strength in some of the big cities, notably New York, but at least half of the nation's urban centers had equivalent Republican machines. There was always a Democratic nucleus everywhere, even in rock-ribbed Republican New England.

If the Republican Administration in Washington had been particularly notorious in its corruption as it was in the 1880's or split into factions as it was in 1912, the Democrats could carry enough states to muster an electoral college majority. In other campaigns, farm and industrial discontent could bring the Democratic popular vote reasonably close, but not up to, a popular majority. It was an even larger protest vote in 1932, against Depression conditions, that brought Roosevelt's first victory without a thought by the voters of a permanent change in party ties.

To the strength the Democrats had had in past years there were added in 1936 the following assets:

1. The almost unanimous support of organized labor, which was on its greatest upswing in strength as a result of the collective bargaining rights written into the New Deal's Wagner Labor Relations Act, first of its kind in the nation's history.

2. A majority of the nation's farmers, many more in number then than now, who had voted against Hoover and the Republicans in 1932 in protest against the collapse of agricultural prices and markets, and who voted in 1936 in appreciation of and for the continuation of government price supports and subsidies of the kind invented by the New Dealers.

3. Northern Negroes, never before attracted by the Democrats in national elections because of the party's Southern orientation, but whose problems in employment and housing were getting substantial attention from the New Deal.

4. Women voters, previously barely tolerated in political organization and government administration after they obtained suffrage in 1920, who were attracted by the New Deal's interest in them. Secretary of Labor Frances Perkins was the first woman to sit in the Cabinet; there were others in sub-Cabinet posts and in the hierarchy of the Democratic National Committee. Mrs. Roosevelt herself was a symbol, active in everything everywhere, and always to be relied upon to bring matters of particular interest to women to the attention of the President himself.

5. The nation's intellectuals, attracted to the Democrats by the Roosevelt concept of the professor-staffed Brain Trust and by the Administration's willingness to entrust administrative tasks also to the nonprofessional politician and public servant. As in the later Kennedy Administration, they were influential beyond their actual number because of their access to the organs of public opinion. No previous administration had dared entrust problems of government to other than the "practical men" of business and politics.

6. Old-time liberals, from Republican Senator George W. Norris of Nebraska and his Midwestern followers, to David Dubinsky of the garment trades, who led a large number of Socialists out of that party into the Roosevelt camp. This group saw the New Deal as a more effective machine for their programs.

7. The long-standing enemy of the liberal—the American Communist—who swung into the united front for the duration of the 1936 campaign on orders from abroad.

Finally, in addition to the easily identifiable groups listed above, were the great unorganized, young and old, who had seldom bothered to vote on Election Day because the two parties looked too much alike to them to warrant the trouble of choosing between them. They saw the New Deal as different, concerned about them, and they wanted that concern in government to continue.

All of these factors together produced a tremendous increase in the vote cast in 1936 and thereafter that could not be accounted for merely by pointing to an increased, longer-lived population. For years those who looked back at the 1936 campaign tended to regard the Landon ticket as a joke because it carried only two of the forty-eight states. They overlooked the fact that Landon actually received one million votes more than Hoover had gotten in the preceding election, and that the defeat was overwhelming only because Roosevelt received five million more than when he had run against Hoover.

The six million additional voters in 1936 voted five to one for Roosevelt that year, and made voting a steady habit thereafter. While most of the new adherents to the Democratic Party voted simply in response to the New Deal purposes and programs, they were not totally unorganized. Groups such as the Good Neighbor League, Labor's Non-Partisan League, the Progressive National Committee—formed at the urging of the President or Mrs. Roosevelt—provided machinery, spokesmen and ideas to get the most out of the popular sentiment. In the big cities, where political machine captains witnessed an outpouring of votes they had never been able to produce by party patronage, the New Deal approach won a rapid understanding and appreciation. To others, including Washington old-timers, much of the New Deal organization for the 1936 campaign was a lot of new-fangled nonsense of no particular value then or for the future.

In fact, it marked the beginning of a resentment of the New Dealers who had not first been Democratic political figures by those who had always regarded the party as their own. Men who didn't resent a Harold Ickes as Secretary of the Interior did resent the former Republican when he injected himself into campaigning. The same went for Henry Wallace, Harry Hopkins and the rest.

Also, the 1936 victory carried in on Roosevelt's coattails a new crop of Democrats in Congress who were a threat to the continued importance of their seniors on Capitol Hill, who came from "safe" districts, mostly in the South. They and some from the big cities had been elected and re-elected regardless of who headed the national ticket and from their viewpoint they owed Roosevelt nothing except as one Democrat to another. They had a personal interest in maintaining a balance of power situation, with the Executive needing them in Congress as much as they needed him in the White House.

Their feeling that the 1936 landslide had imperiled this always-delicate balance was sharply emphasized when Roosevelt early in 1937 brought out, without consultation, his plan to "pack" the United States Supreme Court. The President presented it—disingenuously—as a program for easing the burden of the older members of the Court by permitting the President to name an additional justice, up to a total of six, for every one of the Nine Old Men who did not or had not retired by age seventy. Even the President eventually conceded that it was a program for Presidential appointment of new members to out-vote the old on the Court, because the Court was out of step with the executive and congressional branches of the government. The leadership in a bitter fight against this change in the existing "balance" of the government came from the senior, best-entrenched Democrats in Congress, in which they were joined by other natural conservatives.

Roosevelt had been pondering the problem of the Court for more than a year, ever since it had struck down the Agricultural Adjustment Act on the grounds that farm surpluses and prices were a local rather than a national problem. It had done the same, before and after the AAA decision, holding unconstitutional every New Deal measure where the Court could find a practical method of undoing the work of the President and the congressional majorities. The archconservative bloc on the Court, Justices McReynolds, Van Devanter, Butler and Sutherland, were joined either by Justice Roberts or Chief Justice Hughes or both, to furnish consistent five to four or six to three majorities over the liberal group of Justices Brandeis, Cardozo and Stone.

The Court majorities would rule that the problem before the

Court, involving federal action, really was a matter of state concern, and not one on which the federal government could constitutionally act; or else it would hold that a state statute involved was unconstitutional because it violated the Fourteenth Amendment.

Reforms they ruled out ran the gamut from a mandatory pension system for railroad employees (federal) to minimum wage laws for women (state). From 1933 through 1936 the only major measures which escaped the court's ax were (1) the President's devaluation of the dollar, done by executive order under authority of Congress, which the Court denounced but found no way to restore the *status quo ante;* and (2) the Tennessee Valley power development where the dams were already completed and in operation. The only thing on which the Court could offer an opinion was the government's right to sell the power they were generating or let it go to waste.

Roosevelt, who had not had the opportunity to name a single judge to the Court, came to the conclusion after the 1935 AAA decision that there was practically nothing that the New Deal could propose that a majority of the existing Court would permit to stand. Committed to continuing reform, with the 1936 election returns registered in approval of his program, he decided to move against the Court, which he did with a special message to Congress, outlining the packing plan, in January 1937.

Many, including members of the Court's minority, had publicly criticized the Court for using its power to "legislate its own economic predilections," as Justice Stone termed it. Yet when Roosevelt sent in his bill, it aroused shocked disapproval, even from many who favored Roosevelt's objectives and disapproved of the Court's judicial legislating. It was argued that even if Roosevelt's motives were of the best, there would be created a precedent for some future President to pack and unpack the Court as he saw fit, with the aid of a docile Congress, for motives which could not be justified or approved. The specter of future dictatorship was made more real for the present by the top-heavy majorities Roosevelt had in the existing Congress, as well as by the new and aggressive dictatorships abroad.

At the start, the top-heavy Democratic majorities in both Houses seemed a guarantee of the plan's success, despite indicated defections. But time operated against, rather than for it. The Republican minority in the Senate—where the first test was scheduled—decided to sit back and not let their opposition rally the Democrats on the basis of party regularity. The Democratic conservatives were against the program to a man, and before the end even as devoted a New Dealer as Herbert H. Lehman, Roosevelt's "good right arm" in Albany, came out against it.

However, the fate of the plan was settled by the Court itself. It decided to take no chance on congressional action; it would change itself before a change was forced on it. Two months after Roosevelt sent the Court plan to Congress and while it was still months away from a possible vote, the Court began reversing some of its most criticized stands. Somehow, by a shift of one vote, the state minimum wage act for women which had been unconstitutional in the fall of 1936 was constitutional in the spring of 1937. The Wagner Labor Relations Act and the New Deal's Social Security program, which would not have had a chance under the Court's recent decisions, were upheld while the Court-packing plan was debated in the Senate. To further weaken the President's case, the Court conservatives decided to throw one of their own members to the wolves. So Justice Van Devanter, bitterest of the New Deal critics, resigned, and most of the urgency behind the Roosevelt Court program went out the window. Governmentally, the President had lost the battle but won the war.

Politically, however, it turned out that the war within the Democratic Party was just beginning. For his part, the President never forgave those in the Senate who had not been on his side in the Court fight. His resentment extended even to Vice-President John Nance Garner, who had not opposed the plan but did not further it either. Roosevelt's first appointment to the Court, to fill the Van Devanter vacancy, was a calculated slap at the Senate, even though the man he named was a sitting senator.

Hugo L. Black of Alabama was an ardent New Dealer who had come to the fore for aggressive tactics as chairman of one of the numerous New Deal investigations of the old order. Roosevelt picked him for the Court not for his judicial talent, then unknown and untried, but because he was a New Dealer the Senate would have to accept—the Senate's long-standing premise being that anyone fit to sit in the United States Senate was qualified, without question or debate, for any other office for which he might be selected.

Then he turned more obviously on the senators who had opposed him in the Court fight and representatives who had bottled up and throttled his bill for reorganization of federal government agencies, a program which brought as many cries of "dictatorship" as the Court plan. The President slowly drew himself up a little list of those who never would be missed (by him): Senators Walter F. George of Georgia, Millard E. Tydings of Maryland, Pat McCarran of Nevada, Guy Gillette of Iowa, Ellison D. Smith of South Carolina and half a dozen others. The shorter House list was headed by Howard W. Smith of Virginia, Eugene Cox of Georgia and John J. O'Connor of New York. These men he cut off from patronage and favor in preparation for defeating them in the 1938 primaries if he could do it.

It was widely heralded as the "purge" of leading senators and representatives who had opposed the President's program. And as both sides prepared for a showdown, animosities grew to the point that Garner reported, from his vantage point as presiding officer of the Senate, that there were at least twenty senators who would vote against anything the President proposed simply because of the Presidential sponsorship. And he was counting only Democrats.

In the course of the "purge," New Deal operatives such as

Hopkins, Thomas (Tommy the Cork) Corcoran and David Niles went openly into the home states of the men on the list to recruit candidates to run against the incumbents in the primaries. Roosevelt then laid out a campaign tour, which took him into the troubled territory, to bless the New Dealer and ignore the man whose defeat he sought. He laid his prestige right on the line. Roosevelt's point was that his program was the program of the Democratic Party and the Democratic Administration; that men known in advance to be opposed to it should not be the Democratic Party nominees.

His theory was tenable, but the job was botched in execution. Voters habitually resent outside interference in local contests. By working quietly in advance instead of publicly, he might have drained away or bought off the state machine support on which the purges relied. His program of setting up a new federal machine stiffened the opposition. He had to drop some of the projected contests for lack of a suitable man to run against the incumbent. In those that were fought to a finish, he lost every one from Georgia to Iowa. His only victory was scored in a House contest in New York. John J. O'Connor, a Tammany veteran who had risen on the seniority ladder to chairmanship of the House Rules Committee, was defeated there with the help of the local political machinery.

The Roosevelt defeats in the primaries were followed by Democratic Party defeats in the November, 1938, elections, noted elsewhere, and the professionals within the Democratic Party took this as a further sign that the New Deal was slipping, that its popularity was a temporary phenomenon which would pass with the ending of Roosevelt's second term, after which government and politics could return to normal. The same developments just stiffened Roosevelt's determination to make the New Deal a continuing affair, widening the split between the President and the party's established professionals.

High ranking among these were Vice-President Garner, who had more than usual Vice-Presidential prestige on Capitol Hill because of his prior service as Speaker of the House; and

National Chairman Farley. Roosevelt had no long-standing ties with Garner and made no attempt to woo him. Farley was different. He and the deceased Louis Howe had secured the original presidential nomination for Roosevelt. Farley had stood up loyally under political attack really aimed at Roosevelt; had been director-general of the 1936 campaign, had worked *for* the Court-packing plan, but had kept clear of real involvement in the purge, constantly warning the President that it was bound to fail. Farley's approach was usually practical and political, with less consciousness of the ideological. While Farley had friends at all levels in the Democratic Party in the nation, his Washington intimates were not the New Dealers but the established hierarchy of the Senate and the House and the national committee. Farley's loyalty encompassed both them and the President, but not Ickes or Hopkins or Corcoran and so forth.

Roosevelt, coming to the conclusion that Farley's value to him on the Washington scene was waning, urged the national chairman, who was also Postmaster General, to develop his own political future by running for Governor of New York, Farley's home state as it was Roosevelt's. But Farley was not interested—claimed he couldn't afford it financially—and when Roosevelt renewed the suggestion, it started the notion in Farley that Roosevelt was trying to get rid of him. It seemed to the author, at the time, that if Farley had ambitions for the Presidency, the more established path for him was via the Governorship of New York, rather than the Postmaster Generalship or the national chairmanship. But Farley didn't view it that way. When he decided to remain on the Washington scene, Roosevelt shrugged his shoulders and counted Farley out of his circle of intimate advisers thereafter.

Political feuding was not the only New Deal ailment which made headlines and added to the picture of disorder and confusion. Organized labor, united for Roosevelt in 1936, had become a house divided immediately thereafter. The more aggressive of a new crop of labor leaders swung into line with the pugnacious John L. Lewis of the mine workers to organize industry along industrial rather than craft union lines. They did so in the face of unyielding opposition of the leaders of the older craft unions which had always been the mainstay of the American Federation of Labor.

The rebel group did so as a Committee on Industrial Organization of the AF of L, and when threatened with expulsion for defiance of AFL policy, walked out to form the Congress of Industrial Organizations. Either way, the initials spelled CIO, and jurisdictional conflicts with the AFL were frequent, bitter and bloody.

The CIO also developed the technique—new to America—of the sit-down strike. Union men, instead of walking out of a plant and picketing, sat down, en masse, at their jobs, and prevented management from entering. To many businessmen, to ordinary citizens who could not condone violence, to a substantial bloc in Congress, this was plain confiscation of property by labor, condoned by government. For the first time, every strike, every labor dispute, had become government business because under the Wagner Act, all decisions in union-management or union *vs.* union disputes, landed in the lap of the new National Labor Relations Board.

The NLRB, like other New Deal administrative agencies less consistently in the headlines, handed down broad new rulings in its pioneering ventures. It seemed to many as if the power to pass laws and make public policy had been shifted from the elected Congress to appointed commissions and boards. In Congress the cries were heard that the administrative agencies were part of a bureaucratic dictatorship.

Business and the press—which itself for the first time was subject to unionization of its news departments—charged the Administration with responsibility for letting labor run wild, and they found a receptive audience in Congress. Most of the Southern Democrats were conservative in domestic policies, probusiness rather than prolabor or even neutral. The Republicans were equally so. The furor over labor's use of its new-found power served to draw the congressional Republicans and Southern Democrats together. This became particularly true after the election of 1938, when between them they could muster a working majority in either or both houses of Congress.

This partnership ripened and lasted, controlling every Congress thereafter with two exceptions. The Eightieth Congress elected in 1946 had straight Republican majorities in both houses. The Congress elected with Lyndon Johnson in 1964 had so few Republicans that even in partnership with the Southern conservatives, they were outnumbered by the Great Society newcomers. In the 83rd Congress, which the Republicans controlled by a narrow margin, the coalition still functioned and strengthened the GOP grip.

In the partnership's most obvious manifestation over the years from 1938 on, the Southerners joined the Republicans in fighting and blocking "liberal" legislation in economic fields, in return for Republican unity with them in blocking or softening integrationist, pro-Negro bills. In the period from 1938 through 1940 the coalition did not function in the field of foreign policy, with the Southerners consistent supporters of an internationalist point of view, regardless of what the Republicans did. Still another burr under the Democratic donkey's saddle was the rise in activity and notoriety of the American Communists, divided then as later into separate espionage and propaganda cadres. The espionage activities were not confirmed until years later, but the accusations that they existed and thrived on New Deal coddling were just as vehement as if proof had existed.

The propaganda activities were as open as the espionage side was secret. America was told that the great world battle of the day was between Communism and Fascism; that Communism was peace-minded and utopian in its goal, while Fascism was all that was evil. The civil war in Spain was used to point up the issue and divide the American public, with many of the "liberals" unhappy about an American noninterventionist position, which operated in favor of the Fascists. Also, Communist leadership at the top level in several of the CIO unions was apparent, with little effort at disguise, giving an opportunity for charges that the whole CIO was Communist-dominated and that the sit-down strike was nothing but a dirty Commie revolutionary trick.

In New York, Labor's Non-Partisan League had established its only organized political party, the American Labor Party, and the Communist infiltration of the ALP was early and extensive. As soon as the Communists realized the party was being formed, they dropped their usual practice of running a candidate for Governor. This would, they knew, cost them their legal standing as a party, but they wanted that so that they could then enrol their faithful in the new party being formed.

The official leadership of the new ALP contained a number of old-time Socialists who knew the Communists at a glance. From 1938 through 1940 local headlines told of fist-fights and riots as the two groups struggled for physical control of the platforms at party conventions. The Communists never represented more than 20 per cent of the voting strength of the ALP, but, thoroughly drilled and militant, they were able to win control of the New York City machinery. Only the state committee, stacked in favor of the right-wingers by representation rules, kept the party from being taken over in its entirety by the Communists.

The fact that the men who had founded the ALP were the bitterest anti-Communists of all, with their hatred based on bloody battles for control of the garment trade unions, did not prevent the opposition from denouncing the ALP as still another New Deal idea that savored of Communism.

And then there were America's Irish Catholics, for decades the bulwark of the Democratic Party in the nation's biggest cities. Among them the charge that their party had been infiltrated and turned over to the Communists by the New Dealers had a potency which could not be ignored. Their church was a leader in the fight against world Communism, and American Catholic clerics, with few exceptions, regarded Communism also as a dangerous internal force in America, to be fought at all times on all levels.

Thus as the Democratic Party chiefs looked ahead to 1940, they had many reminders of threats to victory, and until the convention itself, had no guarantee who their candidate would be.

4 The Buildup: The Republicans

Many people who knew Wendell Willkie thought of him as a possible candidate for public office, but there were three who did something about it. Their program was carried on carefully and quietly for nine months before emerging in broad daylight as his campaign for the Republican presidential nomination. By that time the inner circle of Willkie-for-President workers included a dozen others, recruited en route.

In the beginning the concept that the Republicans could run a Democrat as their nominee for President was so farfetched as to be staggering. It involved getting the principal men and women of the Republican Party, who would be the ones to go as delegates to a national convention, to put aside considerations of party loyalty and service and pick a corporation executive emanating from one of the most vulnerable segments of the big business community.

One of the original triumvirate, Frank Altschul, broached the subject to Kenneth F. Simpson, the Republican National Committeeman from New York, in September 1939, three-quarters of a year before the nomination would be made. Altschul was the wealthy and influential head of an international banking firm. Simpson was an imaginative and mercurial party boss who had first sponsored Tom Dewey for elective office and then split bitterly with him. For that reason alone he should have welcomed the Willkie candidacy as his best alternative to Dewey—which he eventually did. But his original reaction was a recital of how the idea would be received in his clubhouse, which he never went to anyhow.

His monologue, as recalled by Altschul, ran along as follows:

"So I am supposed to go back to the clubhouse and tell the boys that we will all have to pull together now to get the nomination for Wendell Willkie. They'll ask me 'Willkie, who's Willkie?' And I'll tell them he's the President of the Commonwealth & Southern.

"The next question will be, 'Where does that railroad go to?' And I will explain that it isn't a railroad, it's a public utility holding company. Then they will look at me sadly and say, 'Ken, we always have thought you were a little erratic, but now we know you are just plain crazy.'

"And that," added Simpson "would be without my even getting to mention that he's a Democrat."

Willkie was not as unknown as Simpson painted, and Simpson knew it. For five years Willkie had been one of the leaders of the public utility companies in their battle against the TVA, the federal government's first big venture into the electric power business. Harnessing the rapid-flowing Tennessee River to produce electricity had been dreamed of even before World War I—now the New Deal was taking on the job of revamping the whole Tennessee Valley through a new governmental form known as the Tennessee Valley Authority.

In a running series of court battles, the utilities lost out in efforts to have the whole program called unconstitutional. Possibly if the huge dams on the Tennessee had not already been built, the Supreme Court would have ruled them out the way it had other New Deal acts. As it was, the Court ruled that the government could sell the power the manmade waterfalls created.

Willkie played a key propaganda role in the second round of the fight.

Vandenberg of Michigan. The Senator in the days when his viewpoint was local, rather than international.

Father Charles E. Coughlin, founder of the Union for Social Justice, attacks the Roosevelt Administration.

Mr. District Attorney. Tom Dewey announces one of the series of indictments which brought him fame as a prosecutor, and later presidential nomination.

Mr. Republican. Senator Robert A. Taft of Ohio, in 1940 a first term Senator, but already a presidential possibility.

FDR battles for leadership. The President in Georgia to "purge" Senator Walter F. George by nominating Lawrence F. Camp, shown with him.

The President as world leader. FDR at microphones for a Presidential White House "fireside chat," warning of aims of European dictators.

Joe and Alf. National Chairman for 1940, Joseph W. Martin, Jr., talks with Alfred M. Landon of Kansas, the 1936 nominee.

Herbert Hoover. The former President argues against America supplying arms to either side in World War II.

Farley concedes. The National Chairman moves to make the third-term nomination of FDR unanimous after his defeat on the roll call at Chicago.

The candidate confers. Willkie with Governor Harold Stassen of Minnesota and Governor George Wilson of Iowa, at Republican Governors Conference in Des Moines, Iowa.

Willkie the target. The candidate is hit by an egg at Chicago's La Salle Street Station.

Cactus Jack goes home. John Nance Garner in Washington goes back to Uvalde, Texas, and twenty-seven years of retirement.

The Lone Eagle. Charles A. Lindbergh, from his knowledge of air power, sees Hitler a winner. Addresses Chicago America First rally with General Robert E. Wood and Mrs. Jeannette Fairbanks, chairman of the American First Movement.

John L. Lewis. The biggest man in labor.

While the TVA was a popular idea, and the utility business as a whole was in disrepute, Willkie's network showed up consistently in a more favorable light than any other, because its rates to consumers were lower and it had abjured phony stock issues and other management devices for milking the companies. Yet it was the Commonwealth & Southern whose operating subsidiaries were in Tennessee and were to be hit the hardest by subsidized government competition.

So when Willkie demanded that the government buy out his company rather than engage in wasteful competition with it, he had a defensible and well-publicized position. The Tennessee Valley Authority offered him $55 million for the power lines in Tennessee, and Willkie held out for more. When the government and he settled for a price of $80 million in February, 1939, there was enough to pay off the bonded debt and give the stockholders some cash for good will. By having fought the government and come out ahead, he became a minor hero to government-harrassed Republican businessmen as well as to the financial houses in Wall Street.

It was just after the TVA settlement that Willkie's name was first mentioned for President in a publication read by the nation's politicians, the Washington column of Arthur Krock, the "typewriter statesman" of *The New York Times.* Krock, with heavy-handed jocularity, reported the fancied conversation of Washington seers looking forward to 1940 and evaluating sure entries as well as dark horses in the presidential race. He quoted one as follows:

> There's this fellow Willkie. He owns two farms and works them. That's ominous. And being from Indiana and a lawyer by profession, there isn't any doubt that he's a presidential candidate. He'll have to go down as the darkest horse in the stable, for 1940 will be a little early to bring out a utility man. But if anybody like that can be put over, I'd watch Willkie. He still has his hair cut country style.

Even a year earlier Willkie had shown himself a man who could handle himself well in public. There was a radio debate on public versus private power development in which he shared the spotlight with Robert Jackson, a leading New Dealer who a decade later was to take a leave of absence from his post on the United States Supreme Court to become the American prosecutor at the Nuremberg trials.

The debate, sponsored by America's *Town Meeting of the Air*—then the leading outlet for panel discussions—received widespread attention because of Jackson, rather than Willkie. Jackson's appearance was interpreted as a buildup, at Franklin Roosevelt's command, so that Jackson could run for Governor of New York that fall. If elected, he would be Roosevelt's first choice to succeed himself as President in 1940. Jackson was not a pushover, and in cold type, both speeches read persuasively, but Willkie's personality sang out over the airwaves and Jackson's did not. His boom for elective office died aborning, and Willkie walked off with the honors.

The Krock column which followed this by a year was not the planted trial balloon that some in retrospect thought it had been, for it preceded by at least six months the inception of the presidential drive for Willkie's nomination.

The originator of this was Russell Davenport, a brilliant journalist and publicist who was managing editor of *Fortune*, the corporation-oriented magazine in Henry R. Luce's publishing empire. He met Willkie casually in the course of the handling by *Fortune* of one of its typical articles on big business, in this case the Commonwealth & Southern.

Fortune had an annual promotion stunt, the Fortune Round Table, held in Stockbridge, Massachusetts. Davenport, in charge, invited Willkie as a panelist and in the intimacy of the setting each was impressed with the other's charm and capacity. They emerged firm, close friends.

It was at the dinner table in Davenport's fashionable East End Avenue apartment in Manhattan that Davenport first suggested, in the summer of 1939, that Willkie take himself seriously as a presidential possibility. He offered to do what he could to make it happen, and Willkie told him to go ahead.

The next aboard the one-man bandwagon was of tremendous value. Charlton MacVeagh, a rising young figure in J. P. Morgan and Company, though a success in finance, had other interests which several times detached him from Wall Street. At the age of thirty-eight, he had already established himself as a minor poet and philosopher and also as a politician with a wide range of acquaintances at the national level. He made his political contacts in 1936 when John D. M. Hamilton became Republican National Chairman to run the Landon campaign. MacVeagh, a friend, quit the job at Morgan's to become Hamilton's first assistant, getting to know political figures from coast to coast.

By 1939 MacVeagh, in the publishing business, had come to know Willkie and had succumbed to his magic as Davenport had. When MacVeagh broached the subject of the Presidency, Willkie said:

"Russ Davenport is doing something along those lines. Why don't the two of you get together?"

MacVeagh did just that, and also, knowing the need for money, brought in Altschul. Frank Altschul was familiar with the higher levels of political operations, though never interested in politics for himself. His sister Edith was the wife of Herbert H. Lehman, the fellow-banker who was the Democratic Governor of New York. Altschul was a Republican who had served as vice-chairman of the Republican National Finance Committee in the 1936 campaign, where MacVeagh and he had worked together. A consistently large contributor of his own funds to politics, he made the Willkie cause his own.

The trio set up a rough division of the labors ahead. Davenport, the only one who ever became publicly identified with the Willkie drive in the preconvention period, took care of publicity and public relations; MacVeagh used his national connections to do political spadework; while Altschul gave money of his own, raised other funds and recruited support from big business and high finance. His own wide field of friendship, and the respect with which his firm, Lazard Frères, was regarded in the financial community, made him the ideal man for that purpose.

Davenport, in his delicate task of promoting the publication of articles by or about his candidate and friend, had invaluable assistance from Irita Van Doren, book editor of the *New York Herald Tribune,* Willkie's closest woman friend and adviser. Though Willkie's election would have forced an alteration in their relationship, she threw herself into the task. She was an attractive woman who ran what amounted to a salon for the intelligentsia and had extensive contacts with news media, as well as a flow of ideas on what to offer. Her employers, Ogden and Helen Rogers Reid, owners of the nation's leading Republican organ, were her friends, and she made them friends of Willkie as well.

Another volunteer was Bruce Barton, whose firm, Batten, Barton, Durstine and Osborne, was then the General Motors of the advertising business. Barton, retired from active advertising work, and a Republican member of Congress from New York, turned over to Davenport his extensive contacts with public relations and advertising men. Before the nomination was secured, more than twenty of them had been recruited for the Willkie operation, each given a specific task, but with no knowledge that he was part of a larger force embarked on a general campaign.

Spot appearances in places designed to do Willkie the most good were arranged for. He was a principal speaker at the 1940 spring convention in New York of the American Newspaper Publishers' Association. He received the much-coveted invitation to appear on *Information Please,* the widely followed radio quiz show on which an invited guest had to be bright to look good. Willkie passed the test with flying colors. He spoke at countless graduations, dedications and annual meetings of respected organizations, all planted by the public relations machinery as some of the meetings where the Willkie gospel, rather than Willkie, was put on exhibition.

The University of Rochester held, for the first and only time, a conference on "New Frontiers in American Life." Assigned by *The New York Times* to cover it, I was on the scene only a few hours before the political connotations became apparent. I turned to a member of the high-priced New York public relations firm handling the press, and said:

"All right, so this is the Republican platform for 1940. But who's it for, who's the candidate?" I accepted, tongue in cheek, the assurance that it was all nonpolitical. Four months later the president of the University, who had arranged the affair, emerged as one of the leaders of the Willkie drive, heading up a Democrats for Willkie organization.

From the very beginning the major objective was to get Willkie known by the nation as a whole, not just the readers of a magazine or newspaper here and there. To do this, the Willkie mailing clubs were established—two thousand of them, all over the country, equipped to distribute locally copies of Willkie speeches and articles forwarded to them from New York.

To another group of masterminds, operating for another candidate, the establishment of the clubs would have been impossible. It involved setting up a national organization, recruiting volunteers to generate publicity without attracting it themselves and bringing the operation into public view. But the Willkie group had an ace in the hole, the nationwide electric utility business loosely linked through the Edison Electric Institute, its trade organization.

After Willkie became the Republican candidate, the Democratic opposition charged that Willkie's nomination had been engineered by the public utility combine. This was not entirely accurate, and they had no proof for what accuracy the charge did contain. It was only decades later that Fred Smith, a highly professional PR man recruited by Barton, admitted to me that the cadres for the clubs had been furnished by the local power company in each city.

Smith also made it clear that at the time the clubs were created, the utilities were cooperating not because Willkie had been presented to them as a candidate for President, but because he had emerged as the leading spokesman for the utility industry, still fighting increased government controls. They were sold the idea that the credit reflected on Willkie in speeches by him and in articles about him rubbed off on the industry itself. It could be, and was, proud of him when it had few other things to stand up and demand applause for.

At the beginning, the mailings of material from New York were handled by Davenport and MacVeagh and their respective wives and children all stuffing envelopes and licking stamps in the MacVeagh household in Westchester. But it soon became too big a task for the amateur though dedicated handful. By January, 1940, with the bulk of the mailings still ahead, a paid professional staff was set up in New York's ancient and sedate Murray Hill Hotel.

To preserve anonymity for the enterprise, MacVeagh set up shop in a room on one floor, Davenport on a second, while Smith operated a mail room and staff on still another. They shunned the appearance of a political headquarters, even after Davenport brought the Willkie candidacy out into the open in March. He did this by devoting a major portion of the April, 1940 issue of *Fortune* Magazine to the Willkie candidacy. He saw to it that the contents were publicized well in advance of the magazine's own appearance in the hands of subscribers, and the mail room in the Murray Hill worked overtime getting proof sheets to the mailing clubs for distribution around the country.

It was a maximum effort, calculated to attract Republicans who wanted to win in 1940 by an appeal to their imaginations through stressing the need for the unconventional approach. The unconventional approach theme was shrewdly tied in, however, with the solution of the nation's problems rather than Republican fortunes, so that it bore the surface markings of nonpartisanship.

The magazine's effort consisted of three parts. An editorial introduction of Willkie by Davenport; a petition, signed by

Willkie, proposed for signature by the American people, asking for an end to partisanship and politics by the two major parties; and finally, a 25-page printed declaration by Willkie of his own beliefs. It was long-remembered as the "We the People" issue of *Fortune,* after the theme of the proposed petition.

Davenport, in his introduction, reviewed Willkie's career, portrayed him as a liberal in domestic policies and a world-thinker in foreign affairs, and challenged the voters to pick, in that time of stress, a nonpolitician to lead them from their troubles. In his peroration, he wrote:

> The fascinating characteristic of Mr. Willkie's position is that most people will agree with it. He is preaching just plain common sense. But there is a difference, which everyone must recognize, between a *position* and a *political candidate.* To say that political candidates always measure up to the standard of common sense is to say that politics are rankly partisan; which is a truism. This indeed is always the difficulty that faces the mugwump: his position is apt to be irresistibly sound, but the politicians, thriving on partisanship concocted of political deals, biases, special interests and the psychological quirks of various regions, will not or cannot use it.
>
> The objection so often heard that, as President of a big corporation, Mr. Willkie "would not stand a chance," is a case in point. The objection is not at all germane to the real issue involved. It is just part of the political mirage that rises on the desert every four years. The politicians own the desert, and they encourage the mirage because they know that the people are sure to run after it looking for water. A man with a bucket standing close by has really nothing to offer them.
>
> Mr. Willkie is the man with the bucket. The bucket is full of real water. And indeed, the water seems to have been drawn from a real well, equipped with a real windmill, and not too far off. The principles he stands for are American principles. They are progressive, liberal and expansive. One cannot dare to doubt that they will eventually prevail. But

whether they prevail in terms of political candidacy is a question that depends on the political *sophistication* of the American people. The less sophisticated the people, the more naive it would be to nominate this man. And vice versa.

For taking up this position, for carrying the bucket, Mr. Willkie certainly deserves the respect and attention of his countrymen.

This was under Davenport's name, but he was also later credited for putting into words the Willkie thinking which went into the petition, which opened with the statement that

before the political platforms are written, we, the people, have a declaration and a petition to make.

In the decade beginning 1930 you have told us that our day is finished, that we can grow no more, and that the future cannot be the equal of the past. But we, the people, do not believe this, and we say to you: give up this vested interest that you have in depression, open your eyes to the future, help us build a New World.

In this decade you have separated "business" and "industry" from the ordinary lives of the people and have applied against them a philosophy of hate and mistrust, but we, the people, say: business and industry are part of our daily lives; in hurting them you hurt us. Therefore abandon this attitude of hate and set our enterprises free.

In this decade you have undertaken vast new obligations, which we support. But because you have not applied to these obligations the ordinary standards of business judgment, you have lost our money by the billions and we, the people, say: give us a businesslike administration that will act as steward of our prosperity; that will ensure the social progress now threatened; and that will manage our affairs at least as intelligently as we manage our own enterprises.

In this decade, under the banners of reform, you have usurped our sovereign power by curtailing the Bill of Rights, by short-circuiting the states, and by placing in the hands of a few men in executive commissions all the powers requisite to tyranny; and we, the people, say to you: we do not want monopolistic government any more than we want monopolistic industry. Give us back the powers that our forefathers declared to be ours; liberate us to govern ourselves by *law*.

Because you have concealed from us the amount of our real taxes, and because you have hidden from us the real nature of our expenditures, you have specifically usurped our power over the public monies, and we, the people, say: give us as much information concerning our government as we expect to get concerning our own enterprises, so that we may control the vast sums that it has become necessary to spend.

You, —the politicians of both parties—have muddled our foreign affairs with politics, with vague threats and furtive approvals; with wild fears and inconsistent acts; and we, the people, say: give us a foreign policy that we can trust and upon which we can build for the future. We are against aggressors; we are for foreign trade; and we recognize that our own standard of living can be improved only by raising the standard of the other countries of the world.

This declaration will not interest those who regard the United States as a laboratory for social experiments. It will not interest those who regard the United States as a free-lunch counter. It will certainly not interest those who regard the United States as a somewhat impoverished gold mine out of which they can still scrape a nugget or two for themselves.

It will interest only those who think of the United States as their land—a land that they know and love—a land that became rich through the industry, thrift and enterprise of its people, and will never regain its prosperity in any other way.

W. L. W.

In his accompanying article, Willkie penned a potent attack on the New Deal. Conceding that the Republicans had originally started the concentration of economic power in the hands of private industry, he contended that the Democrats had extended this power, far beyond necessary, in the hands of government, and that the New Deal planners now had a vested interest in the continuation of unemployment and depression.

Addressing himself to the argument that a Republican administration would have a tendency to take the nation back to the pre-New Deal days in social concepts, he said:

> We, the people, know that the solutions to the future do not lie in the past, whether remote or recent, except in a very limited sense. What we need is a new outlook, a new way of getting at things. Some of the recent reforms must be modified in order to protect our power; other, new reforms may have to be introduced. For instance, there has grown up a new concept of public welfare. Our new outlook must include this. Government, either state or federal, must be responsible not only for the destitute and the unemployed, but for elementary guarantees of public health, the rehabilitation of farmers, rebuilding of the soil, preservation of the national forests, clearance and elimination of city slums and so forth.
>
> The need for these public works is not unique in this country. Warfare aside, it has been felt and answered by every civilized government in the world today, and some governments have gone much further than the New Deal, without disrupting their economies and without a philosophy of defeat. We too must be able to do that. We also need a new kind of budget, a new concept of the government's responsibility toward the taxpayers. We need a new foreign policy. In short, we must re-design a governmental system that, in view of our progress in other fields, has become obsolete. We do not want a New Deal any more. We want a New World.

This was strong language in 1940 for a would-be Republican. He took two additional positions not likely to win him medals from the conservative Republican congressional bloc—a demand for continuance of Roosevelt's reciprocal trade policies, and a willingness to postpone for the moment an actual cash balance in the federal budget. But they could find comfort in his attacks on the loose spending by the New Deal, its failure to solve the unemployment problem except by government handouts, his criticism of taxes and the antibusiness attitude of the Administration. His views on the development of an expansionist economy which could take care of all of the nation's needs—predating the Great Society by a quarter century—drew surprisingly little reaction.

The overall effect of the "We the People" presentation was to take Willkie out of the orbit of the conventional candidate.

While the magazine was fresh on the newsstands, Willkie told an audience at New York's Town Hall that:

"I am not in the slightest sense of the word a candidate for President. I haven't the slightest delusion about being nominated. To the question whether I would run, if nominated, I have said yes. No man in my position of life would decline it."

This was not intended, nor did it so act, to discourage the men already running the Willkie drive or those newly attracted to it by the *Fortune* spread. One of the latter was Oren Root, a young Wall Street lawyer distantly related to Elihu Root, conservative Cabinet member and corporation lawyer of the previous generation. Young Root, who always claimed he did it without prompting, inserted a small advertisement in the *Herald Tribune,* asking for help and contributions to distribute the "We the People" petition.

The day the ad appeared, the boiler factory in the Murray Hill went to work. By midnight, two thousand telegrams had gone out to the mailing clubs, suggesting a rapid response to the Root appeal. Root was snowed under. Telegrams and letters and phone calls came in from the organized mailing clubs, but not from them alone. The publicity stimulated countless additional responses from the great unorganized upper middle class of America.

From that time on it became increasingly difficult, even for the organizers, to separate the results of their work from the more spontaneous enthusiasm springing from the planted seeds.

Those who wrote to Oren Root were encouraged to organize

themselves into the Associated Willkie Clubs of America, with one slogan—"We Want Willkie." Whatever professional assistance they needed in the organizing was obtainable from the Murray Hill. The movement received a steady flow of newspaper publicity.

There were two reasons for this publicity. One, it was good copy, featuring good names, even good young figures from previously Democratic families, and names make news. Secondly, the leading newspaper and magazine owners of the nation were leaning in Willkie's direction. Davenport's employers, Henry and Claire Luce, gave the support of *Time* and *Life*, as well as *Fortune*. The Cowles brothers, who owned a chain of newspapers and magazines, threw their lot in with the Willkie camp. *The New York Times* and the *Herald Tribune*, while holding back editorial endorsement until later, spread the Willkie story in their news columns.

It all added up to the greatest publicity bandwagon in the history of American politics. As the weeks went on and the convention neared, the problem of keeping Willkie in the spotlight turned into a matter of picking and choosing between the opportunities which were mushrooming in every quarter.

One of the last of these, of major importance, was an invitation to Willkie to appear June 12, two weeks before the Republican convention, before the Washington press corps at the National Press Club. Though Willkie's rating in the Gallup poll that same day was only 17 per cent, against 52 per cent for Tom Dewey, Willkie was on the way up and Dewey on the way down, and Willkie made to the assembled newspapermen his first prediction of victory.

Answering a question whether he really expected to be nominated, Willkie said:

"The nomination will be made on the sixth or seventh ballot and the nominee will be the free choice of the convention. My supporters say I will be the nominee and I think I should be."

He knew by then how much had been done in his behalf by McVeagh and Altschul. Combining their political contacts around the nation with their own who's who in big business and high finance, they had worked as hard at their task as Davenport had in the publicity campaign, with equal success, and with even less of their work appearing above the surface.

MacVeagh had penned for himself a "bible" of the thousand delegates and thousand alternates to the coming convention. It gave the background of each, with the factors—including the friends—that could be counted on to affect his decisions and influence his vote. Harold J. Gallagher, who ranked high in the field of corporate law practice and the American Bar Association and later was Willkie's law partner, took charge of the book. In a suite he set up in Philadelphia a month before the convention, he made phone calls around the country to everyone he knew—and he knew a lot of people.

Big businessmen all over were quietly taking seats on the Willkie wagon. There was Lammot DuPont of the Delaware DuPonts; Ernest T. Weir, the steel magnate; Thomas W. Lamont, the senior partner in the House of Morgan; Edgar Monsanto Queeny of the Monsanto Chemical empire, and many others, even Joseph N. Pew, Jr., of Sun Oil, though as a delegate he had to remain personally pledged to the favorite-son candidacy of Governor Arthur H. James of Pennsylvania.

Few of these men were delegates themselves, but they could bring into the Willkie column whole batches of delegates from New England and the industrial East, as well as Delaware, Maryland, Virginia, West Virginia, Tennessee, Indiana and Missouri, states where big business and the public utilities long had had great influence in the local Republican organizations.

Queeny, for example, controlled more than half of the delegates from Missouri. His support had its origin in his dislike for Roosevelt. Willkie might be a bit too New Dealish, but he looked like a possible winner and any fellow corporation executive would be easier for big business to live with than the man *in* the White House. He was later to split bitterly with Willkie, prior to the 1944 convention.

Altschul and MacVeagh had also recruited a number of the party professionals, men who worked at politics either full or part time all year round. The most important at the start was Samuel F. Pryor, Jr., of Connecticut. On the death of J. Henry Roraback in 1937, Pryor moved in as national committeeman from the Nutmeg state, cleaned up the Roraback machine which had gotten both inept and corrupt by then, elected the bright, honest and capable Raymond B. Baldwin as Governor, and developed a keen interest in national affairs, centering around the possibility of Baldwin for President or Vice-President. When Willkie appeared in the picture, both Pryor and Baldwin agreed Willkie was the better bet.

Pryor fitted perfectly into the Willkie movement. He was an extremely wealthy graduate of the railroad equipment industry; by 1940 he was a ranking official of Pan American Airways. Pryor owned and flew his own plane and made it clear he was ready, at the drop of a hat, to take off the next moment for Alaska if necessary to pick up a Willkie delegate.

But Prior's recruitment was secondary to MacVeagh's enlistment of his old boss, National Chairman John D. M. Hamilton, as a quiet supporter of the Willkie drive. Hamilton was in a difficult position. He was the party's first paid, full-time chairman, continued in office after the 1936 defeat to ensure continuity in party organization and planning. With the power to allocate party funds, he could help out candidates for Congress and build up friendships all over the nation. But he was also supposed to be strictly neutral, never to use his office for one presidential possibility as against another. He made sure that he didn't, but he was accused of it anyhow after his appearance at the convention as a Willkie man.

Hamilton was leader of the conservative, anti-Landon wing of the Kansas GOP, who ran Landon's 1936 campaign because he was a Kansan first and a factionalist second. Personally an attractive, redheaded dynamo, he wanted to run the 1940 campaign and this time to win; so again, ideology took second place in his thinking.

As national chairman, he knew men in each state on whose judgment of local affairs he relied. In Nebraska that man was Robert Simmons, Chief Justice of the State Supreme Court. In mid-April Hamilton called him to discuss that state's primary the week before, in which a Dewey slate had defeated a Vandenberg slate, and the New Yorker had claim therefore to the state's fourteen delegates.

Simmons had a question of his own:

"Who the hell is this guy Willkie? As near as I can tell, half of the Nebraska delegation is for him, no matter who they're supposed to be for."

Simmons turned out later to be high in his estimate—only five of the fourteen voted at Philadelphia for Willkie, but Hamilton became interested. Approached by Pryor and Altschul for active support, he explained his need to stay neutral, and also his interest in a candidate who could win.

He decided he could act as friend and adviser to the Willkie men, as long as he did not use his personal contacts with delegates until after the convention assembled and he laid down his gavel as national chairman, at the opening session. He met secretly with Willkie and MacVeagh and Davenport. Two key decisions came from the meetings, on Hamilton's advice.

One was that Willkie should be presented to the convention as the native son of Indiana in order to minimize the New York corporate curse. The other was that the man to make the nominating speech should be Charles A. Halleck. Halleck, then a young Hoosier Congressman with only six years service in the House, was a fellow-graduate of Willkie from the University of Indiana and had belonged, while there, to the same Greek letter fraternity.

The second meeting also brought the decision, on Hamilton's recommendation, that once the convention met, Governor Harold E. Stassen of Minnesota should be the floor manager of the Willkie drive. Stassen had already been picked, and announced, by Hamilton as the convention's temporary chairman or keynoter, so until after his speech he had to be as neutral as

Hamilton. Stassen, a progressive Minnesotan who had broken the grip of a radical Democratic coalition in his home state, was at the height of his popularity and was the ideal man for their floor manager.

When he did come out into the open for Willkie, he did so in the most effective manner. Still publicly uncommitted to any candidate, he announced he would interview both Dewey and Willkie on their position in international affairs and be guided by the comparison, if any, to be made. He did just that and then came out for Willkie, to whom he was already privately committed.

Although no one outside the Willkie camp realized it at the time, the whole convention machinery was Willkie's. He had Hamilton, the national chairman, who would open the session; Stassen the keynoter; and Joseph W. Martin of Massachusetts, the permanent chairman, while a favorite-son candidate himself, knew full well that he and his delegates would be in the Willkie column after the opening ballots. The permanent chairman could make the crucial rulings during the convention sessions, and as long as he was not obviously unfair, he would never be challenged. Finally, the death of Ralph Williams of Oregon, the Taft-oriented chairman of the committee on arrangements on the eve of the convention, put control of tickets, seating and all other arrangements in the hands of Sam Pryor, the committee vice-chairman and natural successor.

But there was one big hole in the plans of the Willkie group. Apart from Stassen as floor manager and what help they could get from Pyror and Martin from the platform, they had no machinery for operating on the floor during the balloting. Hamilton discovered this casually the Saturday night before the convention opened, after all the party chiefs had attended the traditional dinner of the national committee.

He and his friends in the Willkie camp moved into Hamilton's hotel room and worked through the early hours of Sunday morning. Among those there were Sinclair Weeks and Henry

Cabot Lodge of Massachusetts; Pryor and Baldwin of Connecticut, Ken Simpson and Mayor Rolland B. Marvin of Syracuse, New York; Walter S. Hallanan of West Virginia, and Halleck of Indiana.

Pooling their information from the MacVeagh bible and Hamilton's most extensive knowledge, they agreed on the key man or men in each state delegation with whom they should stay in touch. Pryor produced a map of the convention hall itself, and each man present was assigned a small group of state delegations, seated nearby, as his own to handle.

This liaison work was not only for applying pressure for votes, but for holding them back on the early balloting. The Willkieites wanted to make sure that their strength grew on each successive roll call. They arranged, in their midnight to dawn session, to hold their first ballot total to under one hundred votes, if possible, out of strength that was three times as great. A final detail worked out was that Pryor, on the platform, would have a direct telephone line into Willkie's own room at the Hotel Warwick for instant communication if it became necessary.

The meeting was so impromptu no secretarial assistance had been ordered, and so full of top secrets that none could be recruited casually. So Halleck, later Republican leader of the House of Representatives, kept the record by pecking away with two fingers on a borrowed portable typewriter. The potential delegate total he added up was so impressive that Hamilton, years later, said:

"If we had had Michigan [Vandenberg's votes] we could have swung the nomination by the third ballot."

As the political spadework went on, the Willkie buildup for popular support was nearing crescendo. Delegates arriving Saturday or Sunday for the Monday opening found their hotel mail boxes crammed beyond capacity or belief with telegrams and telephone messages from people they knew or who knew them, demanding they support Willkie. No matter how many they threw away, there was more the next time they looked. It rapidly became impossible for a delegate to leave a message for his wife or a friend without fearing it would get lost in the mess of messages from the outside.

The whole message deluge, staged by the Oren Root Willkie clubs, irritated those delegates not committed to his cause, but it also made them Willkie-conscious with a vengeance. And things were just as bad if they took a walk in the sunny streets to get away from the crowded hotel public rooms and lobbies. Hundreds of pretty young girls and attractive young men, who were hardly old enough to have been to a national convention before, thrust Willkie banners and buttons on everyone who passed.

Many of these had come to Philadelphia on their own, and for many it was the start of an interest in politics that would continue. But a lot of the pretty girls were also receptionists and secretaries in Wall Street banking, financial and legal firms who had been given a week's holiday, with expenses paid, to go to Philadelphia and cheer for Willkie.

Willkie himself arrived in Philadelphia early Saturday afternoon, by train from New York. To preserve the underdog flavor of his candidacy, he came without press agent or entourage, accompanied only by Mrs. Willkie. There was no mass demonstration at the station, only a few well-identified Willkie supporters like Halleck, Bruce Barton and Sinclair Weeks, plus a platoon of newspaper reporters.

The rules of the game called for Willkie to have a prepared statement, handed out by his press agent, with a brief interview to supplement it if the reporters so desired. The book also called for a cavalcade of cars to scream itself and the candidate back to his hotel, attracting attention by sheer decibel count. But Willkie threw the rule book out the window.

"What are your plans?" a reporter asked.

"Right now, since it's such a beautiful day, I'm going to send Mrs. Willkie on to the hotel by car, to unpack, and I'm going to walk there, to see what this convention city looks like. If you boys have any questions, why don't you walk along with me, and we'll talk on the way."

It was possibly the first political walking tour, with the press as bait. As the big man strolled along, talking casually to others wielding pencils on notepaper as best they could, the people on the street sensed that he was someone, and the word could be heard going from mouth to mouth—"That's Wendell Willkie."

Some looked, some stared, some cheered and others joined the procession to ask questions themselves, elbowing for position with the reporters. Hatless and casual, he was like a Pied Piper on the streets of Philadelphia from the moment of his arrival. If he stopped at a stand for a shoeshine, he let himself be interviewed by the bootblack as well as anyone else in the crowd who could push in close enough to have his question heard.

He took street-corner positions on anything and everything—a third term for a President, the chances of war, economic recovery, farm policy, the party platform, his own chances of getting nominated—all subjects normally covered in carefully worked out press statements from a candidate's headquarters.

The reporters had to stick with him, just in case he said something—somewhere—that they couldn't afford to miss, which made the Willkie arrival a problem for them much the way the avalanche of messages was a problem for the delegates.

For example, Taft had a headquarters of 102 rooms at one hotel, Dewey 78 rooms at another, Vandenberg 48 at a third, all with press rooms and publicity men on the job to keep reporters posted, and protect them on things that went on when they weren't around. Harold Gallegher had five unpublicized rooms for Willkie operations in what had been the personal living quarters of the manager of the Benjamin Franklin Hotel; Willkie had his own pair of rooms at the Warwick for living purposes, but the visible Willkie headquarters was under the candidate's hat, if he wore one.

The press despairingly notified their editors that they would have no time to cover the other headquarters of other candidates, that covering Willkie alone was a full-time job.

Willkie carried his meet everyone, talk to everyone performance into the hotel lobbies as well as the streets. He stole and held the spotlight from the moment he arrived. The act was a definite plus, with only one recorded minus.

In the lobby of the Ben Franklin he sauntered over to a group which happened to include a fellow Hoosier, James E. Watson, from Rushville, Mrs. Willkie's home town. Jim Watson, Republican Senator from Indiana from 1917 to 1933 and leader of the majority in the U.S. Senate in the Coolidge era, was a diehard conservative and party regular. To him there was nothing worse than a Democrat as President except a Democrat running for President on the Republican ticket. When Willkie sought his views, he drawled:

"Well, Wendell, you know that back home in Indiana it's all right if the town whore joins the church, but they don't let her lead the choir the first night."

The roar of laughter from all—including Willkie—did not cover up bitterness to be reflected in the balloting ahead.

5 The Buildup: The Democrats

Between Election Day, 1932, and taking the oath of office on March 4, 1933, there was speculation that President-elect Roosevelt might form some kind of national unity government; that he might include leading national figures in his Cabinet. The names mentioned included Al Smith, Newton D. Baker of Ohio, Governors Harry F. Byrd of Virginia and Albert C. Ritchie of Maryland, all of whom had been rivals for the presidential nomination Roosevelt won.

Jim Farley, then in his prime as Roosevelt's political ringmaster, disposed of the whole batch of names with a single denial, uttered for information but not for quotation. Farley said:

"There won't be any presidential possibilities in the Roosevelt Cabinet."

The evaluation was valid then, and forever after. The original Cabinet featured elderly and reasonably competent Democrats of good repute, such as George H. Dern of Utah, Claude Swanson of Virginia, Dan Roper of North Carolina; Harold L. Ickes and Henry A. Wallace, independent Republicans; Frances Perkins, the first woman Cabinet member; personal friends, first William H. Woodin and later Henry Morgenthau —not a presidential possibility in the lot. Nor were their replacements, if and when made. The man with the broadest national reputation was Cordell Hull, incoming Secretary of State, who had won that reputation with a quarter-century of service in the House and Senate.

The Cabinet was not the only area relatively denuded of men of possible presidential stature or availability. Congressional leadership had been overwhelmed by the executive tidal wave in Roosevelt's famous "first hundred days" in office, when emergency measures to meet the Depression crisis were drafted in the White House and passed on Capitol Hill in record haste, and the leadership of Senate and House never recovered in prestige. For years they had the unhappy choice of fighting their own popular President and being viewed as obstructionist, or going along routinely and being characterized as rubber stamps. With the new emphasis on the federal government in Washington as the source of all power and money, the normal crop of state Governors who could be presidential candidates—if urged—was less and less in the spotlight, and had a harder time winning national identification.

There were two leading New Deal figures who stood out, but they were ruled from consideration for the Presidency by circumstances beyond their own control. Robert F. Wagner had his name on the labor, social security and banking reform measures of the New Deal, as well as many others, but he had been born abroad, did not meet the constitutional requirement that the President be a natural-born, rather than naturalized citizen. Then there was Herbert H. Lehman, whom Roosevelt had dubbed "my good right arm" when they were in Albany together, and who was now operating "the Little New Deal" in the New York state capital. But Lehman was Jewish, and no one of his faith had ever been seriously considered for President.

Roosevelt himself, in his second term, gave thought to two others who might succeed him when 1940 came around. The first was Robert Jackson, the Solicitor General, who later was Attorney General, Justice of the United States Supreme Court, and chief American prosecutor at the Nuremberg war crimes trials that followed World War II. Roosevelt toyed with sponsoring Jackson for Governor of New York to succeed Lehman, not anxious for another, fourth term. If that was successfully accomplished, Jackson, Protestant, liberal, New Dealer, could be pushed for the Presidency. But those in New York who had other ideas about the governorship kept bringing up and even overstating the extent of Jackson's relatively poor showing in the 1938 *Town Meeting of the Air* debate with the then lesser-known Wendell Willkie, and Jackson dropped out of contention.

The President then turned his thoughts toward Harry Hopkins. A poor boy from Iowa who matured as a social worker, Hopkins then took on the job for government of keeping people from starving by means of WPA jobs. He had started out as completely apolitical, but by 1939 he was Roosevelt's chief personal agent in both politics and government, as close to him as only Louis Howe, Roosevelt's original Albany mentor, had been. Hopkins even lived in the White House, with access to the President night and day. His dedication to the President and the New Deal was beyond question. Hopkins was unpopular in the party, having acted for Roosevelt, even as his hatchet man, without regard for personal consequences. The President would have met with rabid opposition in seeking the Democratic presidential nomination for Hopkins, but the matter became moot. Hopkins' precarious health worsened and his life, rather than his candidacy, was in question.

Thus, in 1939, when the question of a nominee for 1940 became timely, there was not a single obvious outstanding successor to Roosevelt in sight. It was taken for granted that the nominee would have to have Roosevelt's own blessings, not only to win the nomination but the election. The speculation that went on and on in the perpetual Washington boom and rumor factory therefore included men who were not so obvious, not so outstanding, or else men with both reputations and handicaps established in advance. The list included:

1. Cordell Hull, still the Secretary of State, who had added to his prestige in that post—no mean feat in the light of the President's tendency to run the nation's foreign affairs himself. But Hull had been born in 1871 and would be seventy when Roosevelt's second term ended, older than any newcomer who had ever entered the White House.

2. John Nance Garner, the Texan who had left the Speakership of the House for the Vice-Presidency. He had been viewed so much the radical in 1932 that he was kept under wraps—not allowed to make major speeches—for the duration of the campaign. He hadn't changed, but events had passed him, leaving him by 1939 in the role of the Administration conservative. Also, he was two years older than Hull.

3. Jim Farley, who had first appeared on the national scene as the New York state chairman touring the country seeking delegates for Roosevelt's first nomination. He kept on traveling, as national chairman and Postmaster General, had more personal friends in the Democratic Party than anyone else, and had won the affection of the Washington press corps for his candid and realistic relations with newsmen. He was a Catholic, and the memory of Al Smith's defeat in 1928 was still cited as proof that a Catholic could not be elected President. Also, he was not identified in the mind of the electorate as a New Dealer in philosophy, but as the man who ran the election machinery that made the New Deal possible.

4. Paul V. McNutt, a dashingly attractive former Governor of Indiana, who had been National Commander of the American Legion and dean of the University of Indiana Law School. He served in the Roosevelt Administration as High Commissioner to the Philippines and Social Security Administrator, without ever achieving full New Deal identification or winning Roosevelt's confidence. His public handicap was the corrupt Indiana machine from which he sprung politically.

5. Jesse H. Jones, the Texas millionaire who headed the government's original big lending agency, the Reconstruction Finance Corporation. He was the favorite of the party's con-

servatives. They could point to the businesslike tactics of the RFC under Jones as an example of how government ought to operate in business if it got into business at all, in contrast to the giveaway programs of Hopkins in the WPA or Wallace in the AAA.

6. Burton K. Wheeler, long-time Senator from Montana who had first achieved fame publicizing the Teapot Dome oil scandal giveaway of the Harding Administration, and had followed that by running for Vice-President on Robert Marion La Follette's Progressive Party ticket in 1924. He was completely identified as a Western progressive, part of the bipartisan group that included Gerald P. Nye of Wisconsin, William E. Borah of Idaho, George W. Norris of Nebraska and others. But he had split with Roosevelt on the Court-packing plan, and also, like most of the Western progressives, was a dedicated and convinced isolationist.

7. Henry Agard Wallace of Iowa, the Secretary of Agriculture whose father had been Secretary of Agriculture in the Republican Harding Cabinet, and who had been Republican himself up to the Smith-Hoover campaign of 1928. He was later to be Vice-President, and finally a Progressive Party candidate against Harry S Truman in the four-cornered 1948 campaign. But in 1939 he was regarded as one of the most dedicated and radical of the New Dealers, so much so that no one but Roosevelt figured he had national stature. He was under constant fire by New Deal critics for the Agricultural Adjustment Administration policies, which paid farmers not to produce until the farm surplus ceased glutting the market.

It was difficult for anyone scanning the list to pick from it a man qualified for the Presidency, not too old, whom Roosevelt trusted and would endorse, and who would be a better than even bet to win the election. The President himself played the game. In a whole series of private and supposedly confidential sessions in 1939 with friends, advisers and others not necessarily in either class, he would go up and down the list; taking it for granted that he would not run himself, he would review the pluses and minuses alongside other names and always wind up eliminating all of the "possibilities" as impossible.

At the beginning those who were privileged to hear the Presidential evaluations of others felt they were sharing a special confidence. But as these sessions continued, word spread, and the effect was to convince Farley, Garner and Hull that the President was ruling out everyone else so that he could seek for himself the third term for which no American President had ever been nominated. It was not until after Roosevelt's fourth term, in 1951 and with Harry S Truman in the White House, that the Twenty-second Amendment barring a President from being elected more than twice went into effect.

In 1939 those closer to Roosevelt than Farley or Hull or Garner felt that the President had a genuine concern for the carrying on of the New Deal past his own second term in office. They accepted as consistent with Roosevelt's whole record and philosophy his hopes for continued progress toward a higher national standard of living, based on an economy much different from any the nation had yet experienced. They saw truth in his observation that the tendency of the professional politician was to fall back or sit tight, rather than continue to press for reform even after a certain degree of it had been achieved. And they also believed that Roosevelt did not want to run himself.

Samuel I. Rosenman was the almost permanent anchor man on Roosevelt's otherwise changing speech-writing teams, and was as close to Roosevelt as anyone with the exception of Hopkins. In his book *Working with Roosevelt* (Harper & Brothers, New York, 1952), Rosenman took the position that at least up to the invasion of Norway by Hitler in April, 1940, Roosevelt was determined not to run. He gave in detail the picture of Roosevelt taking Sam and his wife Dorothy up to look at real estate for a home for themselves; the plan was that they would all be neighbors after the 1940 retirement, when he and Rosenman would work on the Presidential papers of the New Deal for the benefit of future historians.

Rosenman's belief, based on this and the way the President talked so fondly of retirement, is not supported by other evidence; in fact, it runs contrary to everything else. The President did not lie to Rosenman. He was exercising his imagination in one of his quite frequent flights of fancy. He was also indulging in his favorite device of dissembling. Roosevelt frequently was accused of lying by men who had discussed matters with him, leaving with the feeling that the President had taken a definite position or made a full commitment to a program, only to discover later that he had embarked on an opposite course. They overlooked the escape hatch which the President had inserted casually someplace, and which for the President had the effect of preserving his own freedom of action.

This habit did more than anything else to ruin his relationship with Farley. For example, Farley had a long and serious talk with Roosevelt at Hyde Park in July of 1939, devoted at the suggestion of both to the 1940 problem. Roosevelt, pledging Farley to the utmost confidence, told his national chairman and original advance-man that he wouldn't be a candidate, wouldn't run for a third term. He listened with apparent approval to Farley's suggestions as to how and when he could best take himself out of the race. Roosevelt's escape hatch lay in the word "candidate," to him a man who announced his candidacy and went out for the nomination. He never mentioned the word "draft" and therefore did not rule it out, as he saw it.

Talking then with Farley, he ruled out as he had done with others all of the frequently mentioned possible successors, and stressed the need for him and Farley to work together to make sure that all of the important delegations were friendly, would follow the Presidential advice and swing behind some nominee Roosevelt could in conscience support.

At the time the bonds between the President and the Postmaster General had already been strained, and while Farley took the President's disclaimer at face value for the moment, he soon joined Garner in the conclusion that the President's position was designed to immobilize opposition. Until the President took a public position eliminating himself from consideration, all other candidacies would be on an "if" basis. The longer the delay, the more inevitable a third Roosevelt nomination would appear.

The fiction that the President was not to be considered a candidate was one that Roosevelt maintained right up to and through the 1940 convention itself, long after his own tactics had barred practical consideration of anyone else and made the "draft" inevitable. In the week before the convention, when the only real discussion was over who else would be on the ticket, the President spent time and thought on the wording of the message he would send the delegates that would release them from their pledges to him, thus giving them a free choice of candidates.

Looking backward, it seems most probable that Roosevelt decided to try to be his own successor when the general war in Europe first loomed as inevitable. This was in the spring of 1939 when Hitler, scrapping the six months old Munich Pact, marched his armies into the remainder of Czechoslovakia, which the Munich dismemberment had left defenseless.

The English and French governments, up to then appeasement-minded, understood then that they could never trust Hitler's word, that it was never more than a propaganda device for a given moment, and that he had plans for continued aggression. So they made a definite pledge of armed action if he moved on Poland, his obvious next target. It was generally accepted that the threat would not stop Hitler. It was also accepted that this time the British and French would keep their word, so that the World War II that did start in September, 1939, was obviously in the offing half a year before.

The world situation gave Roosevelt reason to keep his own counsel on the issue of the third term, although if he were not going to run, he had even sounder grounds for keeping that quiet. Once he pulled out of the race, he would be a lame duck, unable to guarantee to the European nations that America's foreign policy in 1941 would be the same as it was in 1939. While he used the international situation privately as the reason not to discuss his own plans, he never did so publicly until his acceptance speech to the Democratic convention.

He used much of his time for beefing up America's defenses, both military and philosophic, for its probable involvement in a world war which he regarded as unfortunate. But neutrality in the face of Hitler did not appeal to him. He embarked on a program of working against the dictator from the minute war loomed. First, he established relations with the Vatican, the first time in American history, by sending to the Pope his own permanent, personal emissary. The Vatican was regarded as the best listening post for international developments in all of Europe. Second, when war actually started, he began his correspondence with Churchill. Conducted on an unofficial, personal basis, the exchange of views and information went on as long as Roosevelt lived, and it was all designed to bolster a partnership against Hitler. Finally, he began revising the neutrality statutes which he himself had signed in his earlier years as President, so that America could, if necessary, send war material to any Hitler-hating nation.

It is almost impossible to conceive that the President, as the months went on, contemplated turning over his world leadership in the battle against Hitler the following year.

He could not rule out press speculation on his plans, but he did use the prestige of his post to shut off direct questioning. In 1937 a young White House correspondent asked at a press conference whether Roosevelt would accept a third term. To the amusement of the White House press corps, the President ordered the brash questioner to "put on a dunce cap and stand in the corner."

In February, 1940, when the question was far more timely, the President told the White House correspondents that he would answer no questions about his possible plans for a third term, that the public was bored with the speculation in the papers, and he would simply rule such questions "out of order" at future press conferences. This device of standing on his Presidential dignity effectively ruled out questions right up to the nomination itself.

The long period of speculation produced varying reactions among the Democratic figures who had a personal interest in what the President did. Garner was completely convinced that Roosevelt would run again and he was opposed to it, no matter what. He was a Democratic traditionalist who viewed with alarm the importance in the Roosevelt Administrations of men who were not party regulars. He based his opposition essentially on the tenet that the party was bigger than any one man and should be able to win on its own, rather than an individual's reputation. He had his mind made up that under no circumstances—even if invited—would he run again for Vice-President; but that if no one else would oppose Roosevelt within the party, he would do it himself by running for the presidential nomination.

Garner really wasn't interested in being President. Over seventy, he told friends the only thing he really wanted was "to go back to Uvalde [his home town] and live to be a hundred." (He died in Uvalde in November, 1967, just fourteen months short of his goal.) Nevertheless, in December, 1939, he declared his candidacy for the 1940 presidential nomination. His friends set out to rustle up as many delegates as they could, either to block a third term nomination or to convince the President there was sufficient opposition within the party to make his own candidacy unwise.

Secretary Hull reacted differently. In conversations with him Roosevelt had made several oblique references to Hull being his natural successor. Hull ignored the remarks, being aware through the Washington grapevine that Roosevelt, in discussions with others, had ruled Hull out as too old for the Presidency. He was also convinced that Roosevelt was going to run again. He aborted talk of his own candidacy by announcing early in 1940 that he was not a candidate and he denied that there was anything to published reports that he was Roosevelt's choice.

Farley in this same period was in constant communication with Garner and had joined forces in the attempt to block the third term. His ploy was to regard Roosevelt's 1939 declaration to him of noncandidacy as still valid. In February, 1940, he told the President that he was sponsoring a Farley for President slate of delegates in the Massachusetts Democratic primary, and asked if the President had any objections. None was forthcoming. Farley enjoyed the idea of being considered a presidential contender, but it was fairly evident even at the time that he was more interested in blocking both a third term for Roosevelt and a hand-picked Roosevelt successor, so that a ticket of Hull for President and Farley for Vice-President could emerge from the Democratic convention.

He was personally aggrieved by two incidents for which he felt Roosevelt was responsible, both involving Farley's religion. One was a news story by a Washington columnist close to Roosevelt who reported that Farley was not being considered for President because he was a Catholic and couldn't win. The second was a meeting he had with Cardinal George Mundelein of Chicago, the American Catholic prelate who was a close friend of the President, at which the Cardinal suggested that Farley not be a candidate but support Roosevelt instead.

Secretary Wallace, whom many regarded as the man Roosevelt would like as his successor although the President admitted he couldn't be nominated or elected, broke the Cabinet silence on Roosevelt's candidacy at a Jackson Day dinner in January, 1940. He expressed the hope that Roosevelt would run, adding that "certain circumstances may develop in which his nomination would be imperative." Roosevelt's reaction was to laugh off the suggestion as typical of Wallace's standing as a nonpolitician.

Senator Wheeler, the outsider in the sense that he was neither Presidential appointee nor confidant, but nevertheless who aspired to a candidacy of his own if he could get it going, gave public vent to his irritation at not knowing where he stood. He told a United Mine Workers convention in January that "if President Roosevelt wants the nomination, he will get it, but if he wants it, he should say so. The longer the uncertainty, the more chaos will be created within the party."

The same labor convention heard the prediction that a third term nomination would result in "ignominious defeat" for the President and the party. It came from John L. Lewis, the beetle-browed head of the miners, who was then the most prominent figure in the American labor movement. He had been Roosevelt's enthusiastic supporter in 1936, but had split with him thereafter, feeling that Roosevelt had not shown sufficient appreciation either of Lewis's personal efforts or of the $500,000 campaign contribution the UMW had made to the Roosevelt campaign. So in the spring of 1940 he was backing Wheeler for President, and trying just like Garner and Farley to throw a roadblock in FDR's path.

The spring months brought forth constant skirmishing between the previous supporters who now opposed Roosevelt and the group of White House aides and admirers who were working, without official backing of the President, to arrange his third nomination. Farley entered and won the Massachusetts primary as he told the President he planned, and carried twenty-eight of the thirty-four places. However, the Presidential agents got busy and reduced the pledge of half of them to support of Farley only if Roosevelt was not available.

The Garner forces set out to get pledged delegates in Georgia, New York, Wisconsin and Illinois, with more noise than success. In Georgia, which traditionally picked its convention delegates by action of the state central committee, Garner and Senator Walter F. George, who had been a prominent target of Roosevelt's 1938 purge, set about to upset this by urging a primary election. Georgia, site of Warm Springs, Roosevelt's "second home," probably would have gone for Roosevelt anyhow, but Governor E. D. Rivers, a straight New Dealer, vetoed the primary move. In New York, the Garner forces tried to file in half a dozen districts, but failed in most to collect enough signatures for valid qualifying petitions. Where they did get on the ballot, they were snowed under by organization candidates who would be for Roosevelt when the convention came. In the Wisconsin and Illinois primaries, the slates pledged to Garner were lost in a blizzard of votes for regular machine men pledged to vote for Roosevelt if he would run.

By the first of May, the shooting war for delegates was over. There was even a formal ceasefire announcement, which came about this way. Garner had counted on a solid bloc of forty-six from his home state of Texas. When he sought delegates in other states, the New Dealers in Texas moved to get delegate support for Roosevelt there. The truce that was arranged, and announced publicly, called for Garner to give up seeking delegates elsewhere, in return for which he would have the Texas forty-six without opposition. The signer of the pronouncement for the Garner people was Sam Rayburn, later Speaker of the House of Representatives, and for Roosevelt, a second term Congressman named Lyndon B. Johnson. The pact reduced the Garner convention role to that of a favorite son getting the normal complimentary vote from his home state.

The showdown between the President and Farley came much later. In January they had agreed on the date and place for the convention, set theoretically by the party's national committee. The President suggested Chicago in mid-July, and while Farley thought the session might be held earlier to allow more time for campaigning, he entered only a mild demurrer. For months thereafter the two men who once had been so close politically never discussed the situation at all. A week before the convention, the President sent private word to Farley he wanted to see him at Hyde Park. There he told the national chairman that he planned to send a message to the convention saying that he did not want to be nominated, but he made it equally clear that he would accept the draft which by this time was inevitable.

Farley had news of his own for Roosevelt—first that he would be quitting shortly both as Postmaster General and national chairman, and second that even though Roosevelt's nomination was certain, Farley was going to have his own name put before the convention as a competitor of Roosevelt.

The talk, as related later by Farley, was not acrimonious, nor was it a warm exchange of confidences between friends. Both were playing for the "record," Roosevelt to show that he had never sought renomination but was willing to accept it if the interests of the party and nation demanded it; Farley determined that the history books would show otherwise, that the nomination would be by ballot rather than acclamation, as it would be if there were no other names before it.

They agreed—taking Roosevelt's victory for granted—that Cordell Hull would be the best candidate for Vice-President. Roosevelt had already asked Hull privately to accept the second place on the ticket. Hull, feeling it was a demotion from Secretary of State, firmly declined. Roosevelt asked Farley to urge Hull to reconsider. Farley refused to make the overture.

He told Roosevelt that Hull could have been nominated for President, with Farley for Vice-President, if the President himself had not decided to run, and that the ticket could have been elected. The lines were thus settled for the convention ahead.

There had not been for several months any doubt over who controlled the convention. It was the New Dealers in alliance with the big-city machines, all interested in only one thing, the nomination and election of Roosevelt for a third time. In the whole preconvention period, Roosevelt agents such as Tommy the Cork Corcoran, Harry Hopkins and James F. Byrnes of South Carolina—later Secretary of State and United States Supreme Court Justice—had worked hand in hand with Boss Ed Flynn of The Bronx, Frank Hague of Jersey City, Ed Kelly, who doubled in brass as Mayor and boss of Chicago, to line up an overwhelming convention majority.

The city bosses, apart from the personal affection in which Roosevelt was held by Flynn, based their unanimity on very practical reasons. First, the New Deal had vastly increased the scope of government operations, and job patronage flowed from Washington to supporters at the local level in a volume which had never before existed. Bert Stand, spokesman for New York's Tammany Hall, which was hoping for more patronage than it had gotten, told reporters:

"We're for Roosevelt for a fourth term. The third term is all wrapped up."

Secondly, the sentiment in the big cities was so heavily pro-Roosevelt that the political bosses felt that as long as he headed the ticket, anyone else on it, from alderman up, could win more easily. They enjoyed recalling the story of Hymie Schorenstein, an illiterate but shrewd ward boss in Brooklyn.

In Roosevelt's 1936 campaign for President, Schorenstein was being pestered by one of his nominees for minor local office. He was worried because he had received no publicity and no money was being spent to elect him. Schorenstein told him:

"You've seen a ferryboat coming into the slip, haven't you? When it comes in, it drags along with it a lot of the garbage. Stop worrying. Roosevelt's your ferryboat."

A third advantage to the city leaders lay in the fact that organized labor would furnish manpower for a Roosevelt candidacy that benefitted the local tickets. In 1936 the labor arm of the Roosevelt candidacy was still new, still going through organization pains. By 1940 it was accustomed to working hand-in-glove with the local Democrats, and they were used to working with it. In places like Illinois, Pennsylvania and Michigan, arrangements had already been made for the union shop stewards to canvass their members and get them to the polls on primary and election days with an efficiency that the machine precinct captains could possibly match, but not exceed, in their own bailiwicks.

It was not accidental that when John L. Lewis blasted the third term for Roosevelt idea to the mine workers, immediate replies came from a packaged blend of labor and political machine leaders. Joe Guffey, prolabor senator who now headed the resurgent Pennsylvania Democrats, urged labor to draft Roosevelt. Sidney Hillman of the Amalgamated Clothing

Workers pledged the support of his union and of the New York American Labor Party, which he headed; Frank Hague, ever practical, announced that the entire New Jersey delegation, still to be selected, would be for Roosevelt to a man. Hillman was to come even more importantly into the history books four years later when Roosevelt, having decided on Harry S Truman as his fourth-term running mate, told his aides to "clear it with Sidney," meaning to give the labor leader advance knowledge and the opportunity to protest if he wanted to.

For weeks before the convention it was apparent that the same faith in Roosevelt's vote-getting ability held by the city bosses existed in the breasts of New Dealers and Old Dealers alike who thought themselves vice-presidential material. Byrnes was interested, but dutifully stepped aside when he found that Roosevelt wasn't, had other ideas about a running mate. But Senator Scott Lucas of Illinois hoped lightning would strike. The delegation from Iowa, undoubtedly with prompting, named Wallace as its favorite-son for Vice-President when it endorsed Roosevelt for President. Speaker William B. Bankhead of Alabama, who was to make the keynote address, thought his friends had words of great encouragement about his vice-presidential assets from the President himself. Again, this was Roosevelt giving encouragement without commitment.

Paul V. McNutt and Jesse H. Jones each had eager supporters contending that the selection of their man would give "balance" of liberal and conservative to the ticket. They did not know it at the time, but a week before the convention Roosevelt had decided on Wallace. He told only Hopkins, though hinting at it to Rosenman. His argument was that in the entire field, only Wallace was the 100 per cent New Dealer, who could be trusted to carry on in Rooseveltian tradition if he did not survive his term. The others had conservative bases from which they had started and to which they might return.

Mayor Kelly, Ed Flynn and even Jimmy Byrnes were not told of the Wallace decision until they arrived at Chicago, there to carry out whatever wishes the President gave them over the telephone from Hyde Park. They were unhappy about it because they knew they would have to work harder to put over a Wallace nomination, but there was no question of their balking.

What they did balk at was the implementation Roosevelt had worked out for his cherished message to the convention denying that he was a candidate for the nomination. He had drafted a note to Speaker Bankhead, which the latter was to read as he made his keynote speech on the Monday night opening the convention. The note stated the "simple and sincere fact" that Roosevelt had neither then nor at any other time "any wish or purpose to remain in the office of President, or indeed anywhere in public office after next January."

Flynn, Kelly, Hopkins and Byrnes, after their arrival in Chicago, made separate calls to the President, fighting his approach. They argued, first, that no note of the kind was necessary; second, that if it was necessary, Bankhead was no longer the man to read it, since the Speaker was fighting mad over the indications that Wallace, not he, would be the vice-presidential selection; and third, that Monday night was too early, that it would give the anti-Roosevelt forces too much time to argue that the President really meant it and should be taken at his word.

The final decision was that Permanent Chairman Alben W. Barkley, years later to be Truman's Vice-President, would incorporate in his own speech the following wording which had come directly from Roosevelt's own pen:

> I and other close friends of the President have long known that he has no wish to be a candidate again. We know too that in no way whatsoever has he exerted any influence in the selection of the delegates or upon the opinion of the delegates.
>
> Tonight, at the specific request and authorization of the President, I am making this simple fact clear to the convention. The President has never had, and has not today, any desire or purpose to continue in the office of President, to be

a candidate for that office, or to be nominated by the Convention for that office. He wishes in all earnestness and sincerity to make it clear that all the delegates to this Convention are free to vote for any candidate. That is the message I bear you from the President of the United States.

6 The Convention: The Republicans

In 1940 those in charge of a major party nominating convention figured in advance on it actually meeting for five full days, from Monday through Friday. Counting the party leaders and convention bigwigs who would be on hand the preceding week and the delegates, wives and hangers-on who drifted in over the week end, the schedule produced enough trade for the host city to ensure the hotel men, bar owners and merchants a return on the money they had placed on the line to secure the tourist attraction.

The first two session days, Monday and Tuesday, were always taken up with the routine of organizing the convention while warming up the atmosphere for the nominations ahead. These preliminaries included addresses of welcome, adoption of the list of accredited delegates, the appointing of committees to do jobs that were probably already done, the holding of hearings on the platform-to-be, and the making of speeches. There were always the orators carefully selected in advance—the keynoter, permanent chairman and others—to view with alarm the record of the opposition party and to point with pride to that of their own. Intraparty, these speeches were regarded as noncontroversial.

Unless the convention was one of those rare, deadlocked

donnybrooks, Wednesday and Thursday would be sufficient for the nominating speeches—made seemingly *ad infinitum*, and for the balloting which would determine the nominee. These would be the days of factionalism, state pride and just plain noise, of bands that played just as long as the men running the convention let them, of demonstrations that lasted as long as the bands were allowed to play, of shouting, marching and squabbling, climaxed by the hasty rallying of all behind the winner of the voting.

Friday would be spent in picking the candidate for Vice-President, packing bags, paying hotel bills and catching planes or trains for home, in varying orders of importance.

In all these facets the Republican National Convention of 1940 ran true to form, from its opening session in the Philadelphia Convention Hall on Monday, June 24, to the fade-out on Friday of the same week. But the atmosphere was different from that of any other convention earlier or later. It had the most persistently raucous and demanding visitors' gallery, and a batch of a thousand delegates who approached their work with a far greater solemnity than usual. Even when with their wives and friends, they talked as though the fate of the nation depended on their decisions, or even the fate of the world, though many preferred to exclude those portions of the globe outside the Western Hemisphere.

It showed up even in the prayers and songs, without which no convention dares function. At the opening sessions of this convention, Presbyterian pastor Albert J. McCartney of Washington, D.C., told the delegates they were standing in prayer in a "solemn hour of world tragedy." At the evening session which followed, Dennis Cardinal Dougherty, Roman Catholic Archbishop of Philadelphia, stressed that "the great part of the world is laid in ruins . . . danger and sorrow hang like a black pall over millions. . . ."

For opening entertainment, the delegates heard the new and stirring *Ballad for Americans*, given full treatment by Ray Middleton as soloist, the Lynn Murray Chorus and the Philadelphia

Symphony Orchestra for accompaniment. Many felt it was the real keynote of the convention, regardless of speeches to follow.

The skies were sunny, the temperature mild for midsummer. It was good working-weather.

Even without this outside encouragement, the Republican delegates had reason to be serious. The previous six weeks had seen the collapse of all of friendly Europe—save England—before the onslaught of Hitler, with a tremendous unevaluable impact on the American citizen and voter. Four days before the opening session, the domestic enemy, Franklin D. Roosevelt, scored a major coup of his own. He had had in mind for at least six months bringing two Republicans into the Cabinet to be the civilian heads of the Army and Navy. He announced it, as a *fait accompli,* the Thursday before the opening of the Philadelphia Republican convention. Always a master at political timing, Roosevelt outdid himself with this.

Henry L. Stimson, the newly named Secretary of War, had first held that post under William Howard Taft and then was Secretary of State under Herbert Hoover. His prestige among Republicans probably transcended that of Cordell Hull among the Democrats of the same era. Frank Knox, the new Secretary of the Navy, had been the Republican candidate for Vice-President on the Landon ticket four years earlier. He was a delegate-at-large from Illinois to this convention, resigning his seat only as it assembled.

With the Stimson-Knox appointments to the top military posts—there was then no overall Department of Defense—Roosevelt was pledging impeccable bipartisan direction to the nation's stumbling defense effort just as the Republicans were going over their speeches making the slowness of military procurement a major campaign issue. It gave the same bipartisan endorsement to whatever the Roosevelt Administration was doing in speeding up the handing over of American guns, ships and planes to the British—pro-Ally, anti-Hitler moves that some Republicans had already charged were leading the nation down the path to an actual shooting war.

The Roosevelt strategem was also an unpleasant reminder to those about to pick the man to run against him of the great advantage the man in power has over those seeking it. While they can talk, he can act and, if he can make things happen at all, he can see that they happen at the moment of greatest political advantage. On this occasion the Republican leadership mustered what counterarguments were available—Stimson and Knox were private citizens who had a right to act as they pleased; the Republican Party was not *ipso facto* part of a national coalition government *à la* Churchill's in England, because our system was different; Roosevelt's selection just showed that in time of need, to head up the defense of the nation, he had to turn to the Republican Party for talent. But even those who spoke thus for quotation knew that Roosevelt had hit them hard, had strengthened his own Administration at the expense of Republican unity.

The delegates, whether they spent their time in the hall being an audience for the speakers or skipping out to shop and tour, knew from their newspapers that the Stimson-Knox move, emphasizing the presence of interventionists in Republican leadership, focused attention on the party's platform plank on foreign affairs. The members of the resolutions committee were still working behind closed doors to bridge a gap—to find language that would satisfy both those who wanted to pledge all aid short of war to England and those who wanted merely to send sympathy, to deplore aggression and to emphasize our determination to mind our own business. It was stressed more than events were to justify, for the Democrats had the same problem later on, and both the candidates were to spell out their own stands as if the platforms had not been written. But at the moment the intervention-minded Willkie camp ducked a floor fight on the foreign aid plank lest it handicap them in getting the delegates they needed.

Accordingly Harold Stassen's keynote address Monday evening restricted itself in the foreign field to a denunciation of the New Deal for having failed to adequately prepare the nation for either the interventionist or isolationist role. The youthful Minnesotan hit at administrative confusion in the defense effort, pictured America weakened in the world by the New Deal's failure at home to solve the unemployment and farm problems, to end strikes in defense industries, and as generally wasting the nation's resources in reckless spending.

Likewise permanent chairman Joseph W. Martin, Jr., who had an isolationist record in Congress but was amenable to the Willkie candidacy, ducked the war issue entirely in his Tuesday evening "permanent chairman's address to the convention." He invoked the Declaration of Independence, the Bill of Rights, Washington at Valley Forge—skipping Gettysburg out of deference to the Southern delegations—and called on the heroes-to-be of America's future to guide the nation as nobly as the heroes of its glorious past.

But nobody could edit Herbert Hoover, when in his role of principal invited orator of the convention, he followed Martin at the lectern. Hoover's speech reflected his hope to stampede the convention into giving him another nomination for the Presidency. As he rewrote history, unemployment and the Depression had been licked by his own Administration before it left office and only the advent of the New Deal had retained poverty as an American problem. As for recent events in Europe, the collapse of the democracies there in the face of Hitler's and Stalin's tanks stemmed from the long-time presence there of a "totalitarian liberalism"—which he equated with the New Deal here—that had sapped the initiative and strength of the European peoples.

While others outside the convention were urging our involvement to save democracy or fight the spread of tyranny, Hoover took a detached view:

> One heroic people after another has been submerged . . . but the spirits of great races do not die. They will rise again. Here and now America must summon reason to control emotion. . . . The first policy of calm realism is not to exaggerate our immediate dangers. Every whale that spouts is not a

submarine. . . . The 3,000 miles of ocean is still a protection. The air forces, tanks and armies of Europe are useless to attack us unless they establish bases in the Western Hemisphere. To do that they must first pass our Navy. It can stop anything in sight right now. . .

It is nonsense that we cannot defend freedom here even if the Old World fails. Our ancestors, with sparse population and resources for the first fifty years of this Republic, sustained liberty here when most of the world was ruled by despots. We can do it again if we have to. . . . The hope of mankind and the hope of civilization is that democracy survive on this continent. Those who advocate war should never forget one thing. The first necessity of any great war is to set up dictatorship. . . . We should be sacrificing the last sanctuary of liberty in the world in the belief that we are defending liberty. . . . If we join we shall in our own preparedness require two or three years to make ourselves effective. That will be too late. In the meantime we should require the whole energies of American industry to arm ourselves. For us to declare war would do the Allies more harm than good. . . .

But Hoover was for a war on the home front against Roosevelt and the New Deal. As he sounded out in careful peroration:

Republicans! You go into battle for the greatest cause entrusted to the government of mankind. With steadfastness to these ideals, you can put this house in order. You can defend this nation. You can demonstrate that self-governing people can solve the problems raised by the Industrial Revolution. You can restore employment and agriculture and end their sufferings. You can wipe out coercion and corruption. You can make this a classless country devoted to equal opportunity for all. You can build up humane measures of security, of increasing standards of living for all of the people. You can remove their fears. You can inspire their devotion to American ideals. You can and will hold up to a confused world the lamp of liberty.

Republicans! Are you prepared to fight?

The ex-President received an ovation timed officially at eleven minutes, but to those in the hall it was less than overpowering. Hoover's friends from his home state of California marched the California standard around the convention hall, the traditional gambit for starting a stampede. A few other state standards were similarly flaunted by single delegates. No one stopped them, no one joined them.

When Chairman Martin thought the demonstration had run along enough to demonstrate due courtesy to the last Republican President and his friends, he announced that the resolutions committee was not yet ready with its platform recommendations and that the Tuesday night session would stand adjourned. It was the signal for the release of the leaders for hotel-room conferences, for the meetings on strategy that the participants always hope will swing control of the convention majority. Even as those private, always secret conferences started, the situation was as follows:

Dewey, the front-runner both in the Gallup poll and the first ballot support, planned to throw in every delegate he had on the first call of the states, hoping he could muster enough over 400 to attract others to give him the 501 needed for the nomination.

Taft had a solid basis of 52 delegates from Ohio; over 100 of the 169 delegates from the 11 states of the old Confederacy which voted solidly Democratic on Election Day but nevertheless sent delegates to the GOP conventions; plus at least as many more influenced by family or senatorial ties. His program was the more conventional one of starting slowly, building on each ballot and hopefully accumulating more strength after the early ballot commitments to favorite sons or rank outsiders had run their course.

Vandenberg had 38 delegates from his home state of Michigan, and almost as many more through congressional contacts in other states, so that he outranked single-state hopefuls. He planned to play with the hand he was dealt—stand pat and make no other moves—as long as there was a chance he could become the beneficiary of a convention deadlock.

Governor Arthur H. James of Pennsylvania and Senator Charles L. McNary of Oregon were playing true favorite-son roles—no strength outside their home states, but with hopes as strong as Vandenberg's for lightning to strike.

Herbert Hoover, who had buttonholed no delegates, and publisher Frank E. Gannett, who had spent $500,000 on a futile hunt for support, were equally out of consideration as contenders. One had won once and lost once, the other was untested, but they were equally sure losers in the minds of 95 per cent of the delegates picking the 1940 nominee. Hanford J. MacNider of Iowa, former National Commander of the American Legion, could hold his 22 from Iowa on the early balloting, but had no way to avoid getting lost in the shuffle later.

Joe Martin of Massachusetts and Senator Styles Bridges of New Hampshire counted on early ballot complimentary votes from their home states and New England neighbors, with a shift to the Willkie column thereafter. Senator Arthur Capper of Kansas and Governor Harland J. Bushfield of South Dakota planned similar compliments to themselves, but had no plans for where they would put their delegates later. The trend of the convention would dictate that.

Ray Baldwin of Connecticut, an early favorite-son possibility, had graciously withdrawn in Willkie's favor for Monday morning's newspapers, so that Sam Pryor could give Willkie his first solid delegation on the early count of noses.

Willkie, still regarded by the press and public as the outsider, was now the man to beat from the viewpoint of the managers of the other candidates. Until they arrived in Philadelphia, they had not known how much of a menace his candidacy had become. But the Willkie people had a problem of their own.

They planned the same strategy as Taft's people—to hold down strength on the first ballot, preferably to under one hundred delegates, and build the total on every ballot thereafter. They dared not build too fast. Even with a greater vote potential than anyone else in the race, and with all of the second choice votes Willkie's managers had tucked away, they would still fall short of a majority unless they could pick up Michigan or Pennsylvania. And they didn't want to reach their peak until Vandenberg and James, to whom those states were pledged, were ready to concede that their own chances were nil.

Dewey's managers, that Tuesday night, showed an awareness of the Willkie strength as a particular danger to Dewey. Two emissaries went late that night to the Taft hotel suite to tell that camp that unless the Dewey and Taft people got together, Willkie would be the nominee.

The conferees were: J. Russell Sprague, the smooth and practical new national committeeman from New York, and Ruth Hanna McCormick Simms, daughter of Mark Hanna of McKinley era power, widow of Senator Medill McCormick of Illinois, for Dewey; David S. Ingalls, Taft's cousin and political confidant, for Taft. All were equipped and authorized to represent their principals.

Sprague's argument was that Dewey could muster four hundred delegates on the first ballot, and that if Taft threw his strength then, Dewey could be nominated before the Willkie wagon even started rolling. Once it did, both Taft and Dewey would be dead ducks, he said. On the other hand, if Dewey was nominated for President, he would be happy to have Taft as his running mate in the vice-presidential spot.

Ingalls expressed confidence in Taft's own ultimate strength in the convention, and suggested that the same result—stopping Willkie—could be achieved by having Dewey throw *his* strength to Taft, for what would later be a Taft-Dewey ticket. Neither program had a chance. First, neither Dewey nor Taft was interested in the Vice-Presidency. But even if Dewey had been willing, the Ingalls idea of Dewey throwing his strength to Taft was not feasible.

They all knew Taft could control most of his first ballot strength—Ohio's fifty-two and the hundred odd from the Solid South. It was a fact of life that most of the Southern delegates voted as they were told by the managers of the candidate who had paid their expenses to and from the convention city, as well as living expenses while there, and that the Taft and Gannett people had been more successful in picking up delegates that way than the Dewey men. But Dewey couldn't count on transferring more than a corporal's guard of his delegates to anyone else. If he went out of the race, most would go as they pleased, and probably to Willkie.

The Dewey delegates had only the loosest commitments to the 37-year-old newcomer to national politics, made mostly when he was so far ahead in the Gallup poll and they had no place else to go anyhow. Even those bound by preferential primary decisions Dewey had won were not also bound to follow his directions to another candidate. So the conference broke up, with the "stop Willkie" drive as a joint effort never showing its face in public.

Before the various assessments of strength could be tested, even before the nominating speeches were in order, the convention had one other chore. The resolution committee had labored over the platform, and by Wednesday afternoon had brought forth its mouse. The isolationists were happy with the platform's firm stand in favor of "Americanism, preparedness and peace," a plagiarism of the editorial position of the *Chicago Tribune*. The interventionists could point to other language to make them happy, such as:

> We favor the extension to all peoples fighting for liberty, or whose liberty is threatened, of such aid as shall not be in violation of international law or inconsistent with the requirements of our own national defense.

On domestic issues, the party pledged itself to work for:

> The putting to work of idle men, idle capital and idle farms to create new wealth and raise the purchasing power of the people . . .
>
> Local control of unemployment relief through federal grants to the states, but with no one permitted to go cold or hungry in America . . .
>
> Increased security for the aged and jobs for the young . . .

Sound collective bargaining, teamwork between employer and employee, with protection for the rights of labor . . .

Fairness to agriculture, with American markets for the American farmer, and provision for soil conservation, reclamation and rural credit . . .

A scientific tariff policy which would protect American labor, industry and agriculture . . .

A sound money system, with control vested in the Congress rather than the President . . .

Economy in government expenditures without sacrificing the needs of the people . . .

Government job-holding based on merit rather than politics . . .

Equality of opportunity regardless of race, color or creed . . .

A constitutional amendment barring any President from serving a third term.

The anti-third-term plank was a pledge that the party actually did implement when, six years later, it won control for two years of both houses of Congress and a top-heavy majority of the state legislatures. No one there in Philadelphia in 1940 believed it possible, so that the prospect was applauded but not discussed. Nor was the rest of the platform debated. It went through unanimously, late Wednesday afternoon, with the delegates now eager to get ahead with the business of nominating.

The convention rules gave every man placed in nomination the privilege of having one nominating speech made for him, to last no longer than half an hour, and a maximum of four seconding speeches of five minutes each, which, with appropriate demonstrations and interruptions for applause, would mean at least an hour per aspirant.

But no matter who was being placed in nomination, there were chants from the balconies of "We want Willkie" from young Willkie enthusiasts in the same manner that they had screamed "We want a touchdown" the previous autumn. The chanting went on for hours, and at its height, the Texas Taft leader, Colonel W. B. Creager, charged angrily to the platform to demand it be stopped. He accused Sam Pryor, through control of the tickets, of deliberately packing the galleries.

The charge was not completely justified. Pryor had ordered the printing of standing-room tickets to be available to one and all. But it was the organized Willkie youth movement which grabbed them, and—once inside the hall—took seats to which their credentials did not entitle them.

There were traditional rites to the nominating process. A state with no homegrown product, called early on the roll of the states, would announce it was yielding to a state that had a contender. Thus on the first call Wednesday evening, Alabama yielded to New York for Dewey; Arizona yielded to New York for Gannett, Arkansas yielding to Ohio for Taft, and so on. The only surprise was when Indiana passed. Chairman Joe Martin was so amazed that he asked if Indiana was sure it wanted to pass—that it had no candidate. It was not until the end of the call that Indiana announced it had changed its mind—that it had a candidate after all.

What had happened was that Halleck, quite apart from the intense pressure he was getting from the Taft camp, had been unable to persuade a majority of the Indiana delegation—pro-Taft—to let him present Willkie as its native son. After an irate John Hamilton sent word he would nominate Willkie himself from his own seat in the Kansas delegation, home-state Indiana pride came to the fore and Willkie's presentation from Indiana assured. The nominating ritual also called for seconding speeches to come from friendly delegates in scattered states, to show that the would-be nominee's support was national rather than sectional. Thus Dewey was nominated by John Lord O'Brian of New York, with seconds from New Jersey, Illinois, Wisconsin and Washington. The highly respected James W. Wadsworth of New York nominated his upstate neighbor, Frank Gannett, with seconds from California, Minnesota, Utah and Georgia.

There was pathos as well as humor in the attempt to whip up a demonstration for Gannett. His managers had hired elephants and elephant jockeys to lead the parade, but since none of them were delegates, they were barred admission to the floor.

After this came the nomination of Taft, by editor Grove Patterson of the *Toledo Blade*, with seconds from Vermont, Washington, Kentucky and Missouri. The O'Brian, Wadsworth and Patterson orations were relatively traditional. If they varied at all from the norm it was to the extent that they stressed the background of Republicanism of *their* candidates as Republicans, *their* experience in government and, in the case of Dewey and Taft, *their* proven vote-getting abilities, none of which could be claimed for Willkie.

Halleck, having finally decided to go ahead with the speech for Willkie, did it with vigor and according to plan. Meeting the objections to his candidate head-on, he demanded of the delegates:

"Is the Republican party a closed corporation? Do you have to be born in it?"

He dared the Republicans who would be running for election that fall, for Governor, Congress or anything else, to evaluate their chances of election with Willkie at the head of the ticket, as against any other top standard-bearer. His challenge of, rather than plea to, the delegates irked many. Some thought he had lost votes for his candidate, that Willkie could not now be nominated, and if the vote had been taken then, they might have been right. But the strategy inherent in the Halleck speech was deliberate, not thoughtless.

The Willkie people, in control of the convention platform, knew that the chairman would recess the session until the next morning as soon as Halleck was through. There would be overnight for the delegates to sleep on the thoughts he had implanted; another morning of pressure in the form of letters, telegrams and phone calls from back home, from their business associates and their golf partners, all urging support for the newcomer who might beat "That Man."

The demonstration on the convention floor—as contrasted with the balconies—was no greater for Willkie than it had been for Dewey or Taft. It was enlivened when burly Rolly Marvin of Syracuse seized the New York standard, brushed off the fists, hands and arms of the Dewey men, and triumphantly marched it in the Willkie parade.

Willkie had been seconded by Bruce Barton of New York, Ray Baldwin of Connecticut and Ann Stuart of Minnesota, with his manager eschewing the fourth seconder. On Thursday morning, and lasting until midafternoon, there followed in drawn-out succession paeans of praise from the advocates of MacNider, Vandenberg, Bridges, McNary, James and Bushfield for those aspirants. Hoover, Martin and Capper, though assured of votes, did not bother with formal presentation of their names.

At long last—4:30 Thursday afternoon—came the balloting among the 1,000 delegates to see who—and when—one of the nominees would get the 501 votes for the required majority. No one expected it on the first two ballots. They were trial runs —to separate the men from the boys— and the second followed the first without interruption.

The results were:

Candidate	1st ballot	2nd ballot
Dewey	360	338
Taft	189	203
Willkie	105	171
Vandenberg	76	73
James	74	66
Martin	44	26
MacNider	34	34
Gannett	33	30
Bridges	28	9
Capper	18	18
Hoover	17	21
McNary	13	10
Bushfield	9	0
	1,000	999 *

* 1 New York vote for Mayor La Guardia.

On the first, second and even later ballots, there was an incident that irked those who wanted to press on to an undelayed conclusion and amused those who knew what was happening. A Georgia delegate had accepted expense money from both the Taft and Gannett camps, and decided the best he could do was to stay away from the hall entirely. A fellow-delegate, deploring such untrustworthy behavior, demanded each time a public poll of the delegation, which served to expose the culprit and mark him as unreliable for the future.

The Dewey first ballot total was ominously low, lower than even his opponents had expected, and when he dropped even lower on the second—the one thing a front-runner cannot afford—the practical politicians in the hall knew he was through. The erosion of the Vandenberg and James totals, slight as it was, indicated no real sentiment for either outside his home state. With Taft and Willkie on the way up, and the rest either standing still or passing out of the picture, the race was forming as one between the Senator from Ohio and the utility executive from Indiana and New York. The convention recessed at 7:00 and reconvened at 8:30, with everyone having had time for a drink, dinner and preparation for the long eveing ahead.

The Willkie and Taft managers fed in their reserve strength on the next three ballots that followed, with Willkie taking second place on the third ballot, first place on the fourth. He reached 429, 72 votes short of a majority, and only 52 ahead of Taft, on the fifth ballot.

The totals were:

Candidate	3rd ballot	4th ballot	5th ballot
Dewey	315	250	57
Taft	212	254	377
Willkie	259	306	429
Vandenberg	72	61	42
James	59	56	59
Hoover	32	31	20

Candidate	3rd ballot	4th ballot	5th ballot
MacNider	28	26	4
Gannett	11	4	1
McNary	10	8	9
Bridges	1	1	0
	999	997	998 *

Willkie's big leap forward from the fourth to the fifth ballot stemmed mainly from gains in New York. As early as the third ballot, Dewey was under pressure from his New York supporters, particularly those from suburban counties where the Republican upper middle class was 100 per cent for Willkie, to release them from their commitment to him. Sprague of Nassau and William F. Bleakley of Westchester took turns in a telephone booth just off the convention floor, pleading with Dewey in his hotel suite to release the whole state delegation. Dewey held back. He resented the Willkie candidacy as a tide that had swept away his own castles in the sand. He pleaded for one more ballot, to hold the line through the fourth, when hopes he had of getting support from Iowa might reestablish him as a contender. Even as he refused, Willkie's New York strength went to 27 of 92 on the third ballot, 35 on the fourth, and—when Dewey finally gave up—75 on the fifth.

But this, and other accretions elsewhere, used up almost the entire balance of the delegates the Willkie camp could count on. Taft had picked up almost as much as Willkie had from the Dewey withdrawal. Delegates in California, Georgia, Illinois, Louisiana and Oklahoma who had been voting for Dewey switched to Taft as closer to their way of thinking than the newcomer, Willkie, from the Democratic ranks. MacNider threw most of Iowa in the same direction.

With the difference as slight as it was on the fifth ballot

* There was one absentee, from Tennessee, on the third ballot; three absentees, from Tennessee, California and Oklahoma, on the fourth ballot; and two, from Tennessee and California, on the fifth ballot.

totals, whoever could get Michigan or Pennsylvania would be headed toward nomination; getting both would put an end to the need for more roll calls, and all the shouting from the galleries, for or against, would make no difference.

In the Pennsylvania delegation, Joe Pew, the oil man, whispered to Governor James, pleading for James' withdrawal and a switch to Willkie. But James wanted one more ballot, which might lead to a deadlock from which his own candidacy could benefit. In addition, if he couldn't have it, he preferred Taft to Willkie.

There were similar crosscurrents inside the Michigan delegation of 38. Senator Vandenberg, back in Washington for a Congress vote, had told his wife that if the time came to withdraw from the contendership, he wanted the delegation to swing to his fellow senator, Taft. Mrs. Vandenberg scribbled a note to that effect to national committeeman Frank D. McKay, the real operating boss in the Michigan GOP. McKay had obligations in another direction.

When John Hamilton had done an important favor for McKay several years before and brushed off the thanks as unnecessary, McKay told Hamilton he owed him a favor which the latter could count on collecting any time. In the recess between the second and third ballots Hamilton had told McKay he would need the Michigan delegation for Willkie before the night was over. McKay's answer was "say when."

When the roll was called for the fifth ballot, Hamilton walked over to the Michigan delegation on the floor and whispered to McKay that the time had come. But McKay presented a patronage problem which he said had arisen.

"Some of my boys are worried about the picking of judges. They want to know, if your man Willkie is nominated and then elected, whose word will he take on recommendations for the federal bench—the organization's, or those amateurs running the Willkie clubs?"

Hamilton said he would find out. Back on the platform, he told Pryor of the deal McKay had proposed. With Hamilton standing and waiting for the answer, Pryor picked up the direct telephone tie-line into Willkie's hotel suite, and told him of the guarantee Michigan wanted on the federal judiciary before it swung its delegation.

"To hell with the judges, get the delegates," came from the other end of the wire.

Pryor scribbled "okay on judges" on a memo slip which he passed to Hamilton who brought it back to McKay. The deal was sealed and McKay moved immediately, calling a caucus of the Michigan delegation to be held right on the floor as the other states voted. A ring of ushers and police preserved their privacy in the midst of pandemonium. The tally, which was not announced until the sixth ballot, was Willkie 35, Taft 2 and Hoover 1.

So few on the floor either knew of or believed the Michigan decision, if they had heard a rumor, that the sixth ballot proceeded with few significant switches, as if Willkie did not already have the nomination sewed up. The floor caught on when the new Michigan vote was announced. Then came several more votes from Missouri, 6 more from New Jersey to make that state solid for Willkie, 3 more from New York. In Oklahoma, Lew Wentz, millionaire oil man boss, had backed Dewey with Oklahoma's 22 votes without even bothering to poll his delegation. On the sixth ballot, he allowed it to go its own way, and 17 went for Willkie. By the time the clerk calling the roll reached Virginia, Willkie had 503, it was all over, and everybody else started switching to the winner, revising previously announced preferences.

Only those who compared notes later knew how close Taft had come to being the winner. As Michigan started its closed caucus on the floor, Pennsylvania had sent word to the Taft managers that if Michigan swung to Taft, Pennsylvania would do the same.

As it was, Pennsylvania, which had hoped for a key role in the convention, missed the bus. Chairman Joe Martin allowed it to climb belatedly on the Willkie bandwagon, announcing its switch out of the regular order. It was a courtesy made at a time when it no longer mattered.

Governor John W. Bricker of Ohio eventually won recognition to have the Willkie nomination declared unanimous. The final ballot—the sixth ballot revised for switches—showed 998 for Willkie and two absentees. It was the most astounding victory for a man who a week before the convention opened did not have a single publicly pledged delegate. In the contagious jubilation of the convention hall, no one knew that the Willkie push for the Presidency had reached its high-water mark, that from now on each successive development would be that of an ebbing tide.

7 The Convention: The Democrats

Democratic National Conventions always had a flavor and a furor uniquely their own. The delegates sent to pick party nominees for President and Vice-President arrived at the convention city prepared to give vent to their emotions, battle for lost causes, to start a fight if there wasn't a ready-made one they could join. The bigger the brawl or fuss, the hotter the words, the more the delegates felt that they were enjoyably at home among fellow-Democrats.

One long-time observer laid down the rule, based on experience, that "anything can happen at a Democratic National Convention, and usually does."

The 1940 gathering which opened at noon on Monday, July 15, in the old Chicago Stadium had more delegates than ever before—to compete for taxicabs and swelter in the heat. The accredited list of men and women delegates was 1,850, with an equal number of alternates, entitled to cast 1,000 votes in the convention. The list was swollen because some of the states had decided to spread around, as far as possible, the honor of being a delegate. Texas, for example, had 128 to cast fractional votes totaling 44. Enough other states followed suit so that the convention itself, once assembled, voted that in the future no state would be entitled to admittance of more than twice as many bodies as it had votes.

However, overcrowding was not the 1940 problem. Even with 3,750 delegates and alternates, 1,000 more from radio, press, officialdom and the infant TV industry, there still was room for 14,000 guests in the balconies, though they sweltered in the stadium in which air-conditioning was still years away. The 1940 convention was unique because it lacked fire and enthusiasm—the good old convention spirit. The delegates were not eager or uncertain or happy to be there.

The men and women who were going to cast the votes did not look forward to going through the motions to a predetermined end—the renomination of Roosevelt—but they knew they would. They were irritated at and caustic about the party leadership, which they knew they would wind up following. Instead of being avid for the fray, they didn't want controversy, for it would prolong the task and emphasize the job they resented. Their quarrel was not with Roosevelt personally, but just that in his era, past and future, their roles were those of pawns in a world situation which they didn't like and couldn't change.

This exasperation on the part of the delegates was even greater among the senior party statesmen who had something specific to gripe about. They were the men who had figured prominently in the running of past conventions. This time, instead of giving orders, they were getting them. All paths led to a suite in the Blackstone Hotel on Chicago's lakefront, the headquarters of Harry Hopkins. From it came the instructions, what the convention was going to do in the minutes, hours and days ahead. The tense, frail White House aide had never even been to a Democratic convention before, but here he spoke with the authority of the incumbent President, with a direct telephone line to the White House to fall back on if he needed it.

When Hopkins needed direction from the President—who

still theoretically was not a candidate—he could get it, but mostly he acted on his own. His program was to push through the Roosevelt renomination with a minimum of surface discord, no matter how much discontent and griping it stirred up behind the scenes. While he stayed glued to his command post, Mayor Ed Kelly of Chicago, Ed Flynn of The Bronx, Senator Jimmy Byrnes of South Carolina acted as his eyes and ears and implementers. They kept Hopkins posted on developments in the convention hall and hotel lobbies, and in turn brought back to the convention platform the latest word on policy and timing.

Men who still were the public party symbols, such as Farley, Bankhead and Barkley, at first complained privately when they were not consulted. After the first few hours, they were confiding that they didn't know what was going on or what was planned, and that they cared less.

However, the Kelly machine saw to it that there was enthusiasm as well as full attendance in the galleries. Tickets normally handed out two by two to friends of the delegates went instead, by the hundreds and thousands, to the heads of Chicago's labor unions, who in turn saw that the union membership used them. The unionists didn't have to be driven to the sessions. They had no interest in Democratic Party factions or rivalries, but they felt they had a tremendous stake in the fortunes of Franklin D. Roosevelt and the New Deal and welcomed the chance to cheer them on.

Thus it was the blue-collar men in the balconies rather than the white-collar men and women in the seats of delegates who responded the most to Mayor Kelly's unusual speech of welcome opening the convention. Kelly tossed out the window the rule book calling for neutrality on the part of the host, and made a direct appeal for the drafting of Roosevelt. With full knowledge of the Roosevelt message to be delivered later, the Chicago Mayor-boss told the crowd:

> The salvation of the nation rests in one man, because of his experience and great humanitarian thinking. I think I know that the President has no wish to labor longer under

> the burden of this office. He has discouraged every advance I have made toward his becoming a candidate. He is not a candidate.
>
> But this convention faces a world condition that surmounts any man's convenience. We must overrule his comfort and convenience and draft Roosevelt.

There was no protest from the anti-Roosevelt bloc, though they knew Kelly was out of order. They had counted noses and knew by this time there was no hope at all of blocking the third-term nomination. They were going to insist on a formal ballot, after formal nominations, but that was all. As lifelong Democrats who would support the Democratic ticket no matter who was nominated, they wanted also to say nothing that could be used against the ticket by the Republicans in the campaign ahead.

Jim Farley, making what everyone knew was his valedictory as national chairman, set the tone for the quiet dissenters in his address at the Monday night session. He combined praise for the Democratic record in Washington during the previous eight years with a plea for party unity in the election ahead. Except that he referred to the President only by title and not by name, no casual listener would have found a hint that Farley was going to challenge the Roosevelt candidacy with his own, though everyone in the convention knew it.

"When the history of this troubled period is written," said Farley,

> the two administrations in which we have been privileged to play a part will be given their rightful places among the bright pages of national achievement. . . . It is a story of high purpose and worthy action, untarnished by breach of trust or sordid scandals. A program of liberal policies has been written into law, dedicated to the well-being of all of the people. . . .
>
> These achievements constitute the record on which the Democratic party will wage the coming campaign. The choice still lies between a party unable to cope with the con-

ditions and problems of the 20th Century and a party which has made this nation the last stronghold of genuine democracy in a world of violence and ruthless force. That is the issue, and the whole issue.

Having thus endorsed the New Deal policies and set them up as the rallying point for the Democrats, he took on the dictatorship cry which had been raised against Roosevelt from his earliest days in office, long before the Supreme Court fight and revived when the prospect of his running for a third term appeared.

We have heard charges of dictatorship, but actually the total that has gone on the statute books has been the will of the country expressed through the representatives elected by the people to express their will. . . .

For a measure of the service done by the Democratic administration we have only to compare our domestic situation today with what it was when we put a great President into office to repair the damages inflicted by inept and incompetent Republican administrations and elected with him a Democratic Congress that did not falter at the magnitude of the task with which it was entrusted. That task is by no means completed, and when we consider the additional burden imposed by the course of the war overseas, we must realize to the full the responsibilities of this convention. . . .

Under these circumstances, is there a man on the floor, or a real American within sound of my voice, who would be willing to take the government out of the hands of the party that has kept the faith and place it in the inexperienced hands of those who aspire to take control of the government. . . .

Emphasizing that his speech was his own swan song as director of party affairs, he made a firm plea for support of his unnamed successor:

I firmly believe that every member of this great gathering will give our successors and the new national party organization the same support that was accorded the national committee in 1932 and 1936, and if that is so, let me promise you now another triumph next November.

From the delegates, if not from the galleries, Farley got a bigger hand for his show of sportsmanship than Mayor Kelly had gotten for telling the delegates what to do when they already knew it.

Speaker Bankhead, the man assigned to deliver the keynote address, followed Farley at the same Monday night session. His was the task of reciting the New Deal record, as mandatory at a Democratic meeting of that era as the reading from the Gospel at a church service. Bankhead began with a preamble on the gravity of the situation in the world, declaring:

> The minds of the American people are now so deeply engrossed in matters of grave and profound concern, with reference to the preservation of our established order of life and institutions, that they will have no tolerance for the superficial banalities of politics. An election must be held, but aside from legitimate discussions of the records of the two parties and of their candidates and platforms, the major objectives of both parties must be unity and solidarity of purpose in preserving inviolate the structure of our government and the perpetual freedom of its people.

As he reviewed the record:

> No other administration in peacetime has ever been confronted with such a desperate situation as that we inherited on March 4, 1933. . . . The first heroic remedy adopted was to declare a national bank holiday . . . which was the most effective remedy against the total collapse of the entire banking system, although unfortunately, many thousands of them had already closed their doors. . . .
>
> Steps were taken for the re-opening of the yet-solvent institutions and many hundreds of them and their depositors were saved. This administration enacted what in my opinion will forever be regarded as one of the major outstanding legislative achievements in our history . . . the passage of

laws guaranteeing the absolute safety of deposits up to $5,000. . . .

Millions of our people had been robbed and defrauded out of their investments by an unbridled and unregulated system of corporate manipulation. . . . we passed the Securities and Exchange Commission Act under the operation of which those robbers . . . are now checked, restrained and regulated. We broke up for all time the ruthless and unconscionable holding companies . . . plundering decent citizens. . . . people in this section of the country recall the collapse of the billion-dollar Insull utility empire and the devastation it brought. . . .

. . . the Civilian Conservation Corps, one of the most popular and successful instruments of government ever devised . . . acted not only as a medium of relief for the destitute families of American youth but at the same time has been of inestimable value in conserving the national resources . . . and giving to these young men a fine system of moral and physical discipline. . . .

. . . there were 12 to 15 million men and women of employable age without any opportunity whatsoever to secure jobs that would enable them to support themselves and their hungry and naked families. . . . the Democratic administration met that duty without fear or wavering. . . . Every single community in America has prospered and benefitted by this program and the expenditure of federal funds required to effectuate it. . . .

. . . this administration conceived and set up for all time a humane and necessary [social security] program for the softening of the hardships of the aged . . . the rigors of illness . . . the despair of unemployment . . . support of widows and dependent children and the blind. . . .

. . . we established . . . the great Tennessee Valley Authority which for all time will furnish a great vehicle for the development . . . of that great geographical area . . . will be a potent factor in flood control . . . and offers now ready assistance in our preparedness program . . . for national defense; . . . as a yardstick for the control of excessive power and light rates, it has been largely instrumental in

> forcing the reduction of charges . . . of $500,000,000 since its construction. . . .
>
> . . . through the Home Owners Loan Corporation . . . saving hundreds of thousands of our most deserving citizens from the agony and ignominy of being evicted from their roof-trees and firesides. . . .
>
> . . . we have guaranteed for the first time in our history . . . to labor, the right to organize and bargain with employers . . . for wages and working conditions and through the Wage and Hour Law have assured to every man and woman who toils in the industries of the country a decent wage scale and fair hours of labor, and I predict . . . the great masses of labor will . . . not forget that the Democratic party has been their friend and not their oppressor.
>
> . . . at the end of a Hoover administration, the farmers of America had on their hands an unprecedented panic and a Hoover Farm Board. . . . Since we came into power we . . . enacted the soil and water conservation program, lowest farm interest rates in our national history . . . rural electrification . . . marketing agreements, commodity loans; and . . . the immeasurable benefits of parity payments. . . .

When he switched from the domestic record to the field of foreign affairs, Bankhead did some rewriting of history. He recalled the opposition of the Republicans to the amendments to the neutrality law pushed through by Roosevelt in September, 1939, as opposition to something that lessened the chances of America being drawn into the European war. He stressed that the bill, as amended, prohibited the shipping of cargoes to belligerents in American vessels. Actually, the amendments repealed the flat embargo on arms shipments laid down in 1935 and enabled England and France to buy American war materials on a "cash and carry" basis. Even as Bankhead spoke, England could import from America by ship, while Hitler's Germany could not, even if we had been willing to sell.

In a similar vein, he contrasted the Republican record of naval shipbuilding, only 35 combat ships, between 1920 and 1932, with the Roosevelt record of laying down 152 keels for new warships in the past seven years. The Republican record, of course, encompassed the effective period of the 1922 naval disarmament conference, while during the Roosevelt years the construction limitations imposed by that conference, in the interests of peace, were disregarded by all signatories in the new armament race.

And so the first day of the convention came to an end, with the singing of the official theme song, "God Bless America."

The second day began in an atmosphere of suspense. The President, at a White House press conference that morning, broke his silence on politics by telling reporters that he had sent a message to the convention that would be read that night. While the news clicked rapidly over the wires to the convention hall, there was still the day's session, to be filled in somehow.

Two volunteers to address the sparsely inhabited arena were found in the persons of Mrs. Thomas F. McAllister, director of the women's division of the Democratic National Committee, and Arthur W. Mitchell, a Negro Representative in Congress from Illinois. Mrs. McAllister gave the President, in absentia, the thanks of the women of America for building the nation's strength at home, for preparing the nation for defense, for having recognized at an early date the threatening atmosphere in Europe.

Mr. Mitchell, after an ironic description of the American Negro as having settled here by dint of an invitation he was not in a position to refuse, praised the Roosevelt Administration for having let him share, for the first time, in the nation's blessings.

> Under this administration a new day has dawned for the Negro and under this administration have come the first real rays of hope for the American Negro to build substantial citizenship in this country.

He cited in support of this thesis the Administration's Good Neighbor Movement, the number of jobs given to Negroes in the WPA, the money spent for Negro colleges and high schools, the Negro youth in the CCC camps, and the housing projects built or being built in the slum areas.

The delegates, clustered in the hotel lobbies, bars and restaurants rather than the convention hall, were more concerned with the inevitable rumors of the President's intentions. The tenor of the Roosevelt message, by now in the hands of Senator Barkley, had leaked first to a few, and then more got it third hand. Some took seriously the President's "release" of his delegates and wondered who else the convention might nominate. The majority brushed off the wording as of no importance. They wanted Roosevelt and knew they were going to get him. The only question was that of mechanics. Would there be a formal nomination and a roll call, or selection by acclamation? How long was it going to take to get it over with?

That night, Senator Barkley rambled through a dissertation of the evils of Republican rule and took pot shots at Willkie, whose nomination from the ranks of utility executives called for references to the "charge of the Light Brigade" at the great "Battle of Kilowatt." His first reference to Roosevelt, by name, came a quarter-way through his one-hour talk, and it produced the first good demonstration by the delegates of the convention. With assistance of the inevitable band playing march music, it lasted for more than twenty minutes.

But when he read Roosevelt's message "releasing" the delegates as the conclusion of his own remarks, the Kelly machine took over and the delegates were relegated to back seats. What happened was a mystery to the delegates until they read about it the next day.

The Kelly organization, by prearrangement, took over control of the electric amplifying system without which the convention could not operate. The microphones which stood in front of the seats assigned to each state delegation were shut off, so that no one in a seat could successfully address the platform. The microphones on the platform were similarly dead, except the one reserved for Chairman Barkley.

However, the regular house amplifying system was in full voice, and from it blared forth the supposed wishes of the convention itself, its reply to the Roosevelt disclaimer of candidacy.

For nearly an hour the delegates stood or sat as the loudspeakers shouted:

"Illinois wants Roosevelt"

"New York wants Roosevelt"

"Idaho wants Roosevelt"

"America wants Roosevelt"

"The world wants Roosevelt"

And so on.

It all came from one voice, that of Thomas F. Garry, Kelly's Superintendent of Sewers of the City of Chicago, strategically located at the amplifier controls in the electrician's "shanty" in the basement of the convention hall. As *The New York Times* reporter assigned to cover happenings on the convention floor during sessions, I tracked down the source, found Garry cheerfully busy at his work, declined his invitation to spell him in his labors, and reported back to my editor-in-charge. The *Times* story, picked up by other newspapers and magazines, resulted in later description of the stunt as that of the "voice from the sewer." It was also aptly characterized as one of the least edifying performances in convention history.

It was well after midnight before Garry was told that his "demonstration" had run its course and the convention amplifying system was restored, so that the delegates could hear instructions to recess to 2:00 P.M. on Wednesday to receive and adopt the platform. If the stunt was designed to produce a bandwagon movement from the floor to nominate Roosevelt by acclamation then and there, it was a flop.

The platform originally had presented some problems in the field of foreign affairs. There was the same pressure from isolationists as there had been at the Republican convention in Philadelphia, with demands for a flat statement that "we will not participate in foreign wars. We will not send our armed forces to fight in lands across the sea."

The resolution committee, headed by Senator Wagner, was in constant touch with the White House in the days immediately preceding the opening of the convention. If the Roosevelt forces rejected the pledge demanded, their action would be construed as heralding our joining a fighting war at some future date, which would be bad politics. Yet the wording presented gave a commitment governing all eventualities. The President himself, working with the committee by telephone, resolved the issue by adding the words "except in case of attack." It still was hardly different from the Republican platform on the same point.

On aid to those fighting Hitler the Democratic plank was more exuberant but not much more specific than its Republican counterpart. It said:

> In self-defense and in good conscience, the world's greatest democracy cannot afford heartlessly or in a spirit of appeasement to ignore the peace-loving and liberty-loving peoples wantonly attacked by ruthless aggressors. We pledge to extend to these peoples all the material aid at our command consistent with law and not inconsistent with the interests of our own national self-defense—all to the end that peace and international good faith may yet emerge triumphant.

In the domestic field the platform hailed without exception the accomplishments of the Roosevelt Administrations and condemned, as would be expected, the party of the opposition. It was all grist for the mill for the campaign ahead. The only motion to amend had nothing to do with either foreign or domestic accomplishments. Representative Elmer J. Ryan of Minnesota, a party maverick, moved to insert the following:

> We reaffirm the traditional position of the Democratic party as adopted at our party convention in 1896, to wit:
>
> We declare it to be the unwritten law of this Republic,

> established by the unbroken custom and useage of 150 years, and sanctioned by the greatest and wisest of those who founded it and have maintained our government, that no man shall be eligible for a third term of the Presidential office.

Ryan acted on his own, with no anti-third-term support massed behind him, and his move was howled down by voice vote and the platform adopted without further dissent or debate. Then came the nominations for the Presidency. At two prior conventions, Roosevelt had been placed in nomination by John E. Mack of New York, the venerable Poughkeepsie lawyer and neighbor who had first sponsored FDR for the state senate back in 1910. This time the Roosevelt nominator was Lister Hill, New Dealish Senator from Alabama, who made a fervent but brief declaration of the Roosevelt candidacy. Its highlight was:

> With such a man in our party there is no choice left for us. He alone is strong enough to match the strength of America against the avalanche of fate. If peace is possible, and I pray Almighty God that it is, he can preserve it for us and he will. If war is inevitable, he can win it for us, and he will.

This time there was a genuine demonstration, before Arkansas yielded to Virginia, so that Carter Glass could put Farley in nomination. Glass, the aging statesman who had written the Federal Reserve Act of the Woodrow Wilson Administration, had left a sick-bed to make the gesture.

He was both booed and cheered, the latter particularly when he referred to Farley's Catholicism, and said that the few protests which had reached him made him prouder than ever that he came from Virginia, home of the first American statute insuring religious liberty. There were two additional nominations, Millard Tydings of Maryland by his home state, and Garner by his. As the call of the states went on, there were seconding speeches or announcements from nearly all of them, for Roosevelt.

There was only one ballot. It gave Roosevelt $946\frac{11}{30}$; Farley $72\frac{9}{10}$; Tydings $9\frac{1}{2}$; Garner 61, and Hull, despite his protest repeated just before the convention, $5\frac{2}{3}$.

Farley had $12\frac{1}{4}$ of his original 28 from Massachusetts, 25 from his home state of New York, and either single or handfuls of votes from Alabama, Missouri, Nevada, New Hampshire, South Dakota, Virginia, West Virginia, Alaska, the Canal Zone and Puerto Rico. Tydings got $8\frac{1}{2}$ of the 16 from his native Maryland and one from Alabama; Garner had the 46 from Texas, as contracted with Lyndon Johnson, 8 from Virginia, 3 from West Virginia; $1\frac{1}{2}$ each from Florida and Missouri, and one from California. Hull's noncandidacy received $4\frac{2}{3}$ votes from Virginia and one from New York.

Farley's 25 from New York came after two days of fruitless bickering aimed at a negotiated division of its 94 votes, so that the individual delegates might be spared the spotlight while choosing between their President and their state chairman, which Farley was as well as national chairman. Farley wanted 47—half the total—without a roll call. The Roosevelt leaders offered 30, under the same conditions. As they bargained without agreement, Governor Lehman, the delegation chairman, broke it up by announcing that he would not accept a result without a call of the roll, lest he as chairman be accused of partiality if the announced total was challenged. The eventual total was obtained and the public roll call avoided by each delegate going privately to Lehman to record his choice.

In the main event, when the clerk had announced to the convention the result of the convention roll call, Sam Rayburn moved in Garner's behalf to withdraw the latter's candidacy and swing Texas' 46 votes to Roosevelt. Before that could be acted upon, Farley moved to suspend the rules and declare Roosevelt nominated by acclamation. Tydings withdrew, the Farley resolution was declared adopted unanimously and the convention recessed at 1:40 A.M. Thursday. The delegates left the hall as the band played "While Irish Eyes are Smiling," suggested by Barkley in the spirit of tribute to Farley.

Actually the convention's bitterest hours still lay ahead. There had always been a top-heavy majority for Roosevelt for President. Now it had to pick the nominee for Vice-President.

In the early hours of Thursday, before going to bed, Mayor Kelly talked on the telephone with Roosevelt and got from Roosevelt the word that he still wanted Henry Wallace for Vice-President, that there had been no change of plan. Kelly was unhappy over the trouble that loomed, and so was Harry Hopkins, who checked in with "the Boss" at breakfast time. Rosenman reports that Hopkins told him that "so far there must be at least ten candidates [for Vice-President] who have more votes than Wallace," but he added that "I think the Boss has enough friends out here to put it over."

Farley estimated later that there were 17 Democrats of some standing who would have fought it out for the Vice-Presidency if that hadn't meant defying the President. Two of the men with the most strength, Paul V. McNutt and Jesse H. Jones, went into long huddles with their friends and their own consciences before deciding to pull out of that race. Even some of the President's closest friends felt that the mood of the convention was nasty—that there was a reaction against being bossed, or pushed around by needless, phony, demonstrations.

Some recalled that at the Republican convention of 1920, the same handful of bosses who had emerged from a "smoke-filled room" with Warren G. Harding as the presidential nominee had also picked Irvine Lenroot of Wisconsin for Vice-President; that the convention obediently took Harding, but in a reaction against being bossed turned for the Vice-Presidency to the first attractive alternate proposed independently from the floor, who turned out to be Calvin Coolidge. The possibility of a similar, successful revolt could not be dismissed lightly even twenty years later, when the mood of the delegates was the same for the same reasons.

Farley tells the story of a conversation between two southern Governors, chairmen of their respective delegations. Governor

Rivers of Georgia asked Governor Phillips of Oklahoma what he thought of the Wallace candidacy.

"Henry's my second choice," said Phillips.

"Who's your first choice?" asked Rivers.

Stony-eyed and gravel-voiced, Phillips said:

"Any son of a bitch, red, white, black or yellow, that can get the nomination."

Frances Perkins, the Secretary of Labor, who normally minded her own business, which did not include running national conventions, was so concerned with the tension in the air that she decided something had to be done. The idea she came up with, which turned out well, was that the presence of Mrs. Roosevelt, and a speech by her to the convention, would help. She cleared it first with Farley, who gave her his candid opinion that it couldn't hurt and might help. She talked to the President, and he approved. So Mrs. Roosevelt flew out. Awaiting her arrival, the convention stalled through its afternoon session and put the vice-presidential nominating and balloting over to the evening session.

While Farley listed seventeen vice-presidential possibilities, only eight names were placed before the convention and four withdrew immediately. In order of nomination they were Speaker Bankhead, Jesse Jones, Wallace, Senator Alva B. Adams of Colorado, McNutt, Senator Prentiss H. Brown of Michigan, Bascom Timmins, a White House correspondent nominated by a friend just for a gag, and finally, Senator Scott Lucas of Illinois.

McNutt's candidacy could have caused trouble. The silver-haired Legionnaire took to the platform to withdraw, since his name had gone in after he had decided against running. The delegates, grabbing for an opportunity to have something to say about the proceedings, tried to stop McNutt's withdrawal by drowning out his words with cheers for his candidacy. Only with great help from Chairman Barkley was he able to get quiet to be heard, to tell the audience that he regarded Roosevelt as his commander-in-chief.

"I follow his wishes and I am here to support his choice for Vice-President of the United States," shouted McNutt.

Jesse Jones and Prentiss Brown withdrew without fanfare. Scott Lucas' retirement was clothed in language which caused some raised eyebrows. He said

> Had this been a free and open convention, I would not have hesitated [to be a candidate]; but on last evening I saw here men and women and those in the gallery alike cheer until they were hoarse for the great President of the United States, in insisting that he be drafted for a third term. And so, under these circumstances, it seems to me that if the President of the United States wants Henry Wallace as his running mate, that we should respect his request, because after all, Roosevelt is the individual who is going to carry the load.

Lucas' remarks set the stage for Mrs. Roosevelt and her speech before the balloting.

The President's wife had remained on good terms with Farley, even when the latter and the President were sniping at each other, and she began her address with a tribute to the national chairman, saying that "nobody could appreciate more what he has done for the party, what he has given in work and loyalty, and I want to give him here my thanks and devotion."

Then she turned to the major issue, saying:

> I know and you know that any man who is in an office of great responsibility today faces a heavier responsibility perhaps than any man has ever faced in this country. Therefore to be a candidate of either great political party is a very serious and a very solemn thing. You cannot treat it as you would treat an ordinary nomination in an ordinary time. . . . This year the candidate who is the President of the United States cannot make a campaign in the usual sense of the word. He must be on his job.
>
> So each and every one of you who give him this responsibility in giving it to him assume for yourselves a great responsibility because you will make the campaign. You will have to rise above considerations which are narrow and partisan. You must know that this is the time when all good men and

women give every bit of strength and service to their country that they have to give.

This is a time when it is the United States we fight for, the domestic policies that we have established as a party that we must believe in, that we carry forward. . . .

This is no ordinary time, no time for thinking about anything except what we can do best for the country as a whole and that responsibility is on each and every one of us as individuals. No man who is a candidate or who is President can carry this situation alone. This is only carried by a united people who love their country and who will live for it with the highest ideals, with a determination that their party shall be absolutely devoted to the good of the nation as a whole. . . .

Mrs. Roosevelt's speech, extemporaneous and unpolished, had the desired effect of diminishing the opposition to Wallace as an individual by stressing the right of the President to share his burden. On the roll call that followed immediately, Wallace, who needed 551 for a majority, got $626\frac{11}{30}$, more than pessimistic Presidential aides had forecast. His serious competition came from Speaker Bankhead, with $329\frac{3}{5}$. There were $68\frac{4}{5}$ votes cast for McNutt; $7\frac{5}{6}$ for Farley; $5\frac{9}{10}$ for Jones; 3 for Senator Joseph C. O'Mahoney of Wyoming; 2 for Senator Barkley; one each for Senators Brown and Lucas, newsman Timmons, Under-Secretary of War Louis Johnson; and half a vote for Senator David I. Walsh of Massachusetts.

The bulk of the Bankhead votes came from the South and the border states; the Wallace majority from a list that included California, Connecticut, Illinois, Indiana, Massachusetts, Minnesota, Michigan, New Jersey, New York, Ohio, Pennsylvania and Wisconsin.

There had been a lot of spadework by Presidential agents even before Mrs. Roosevelt spoke. There was no public declaration by the President to the press or the convention that he wanted Wallace, but Byrnes, Flynn, Mayor Kelly and Hopkins, with Presidential authority, were passing the word that it had to be Wallace or the President himself would not run.

Roosevelt "had his Dutch up."

He sat in the Oval Room of the White House with a few members of his staff, and as the radio—and telephone calls from Chicago—revealed the resistance to Wallace, he penned in longhand a statement declining the Presidential nomination, and denouncing the opposition in his own party. The existence of the statement was used by the men working in Chicago to carry out the Presidential wishes. The text was disclosed for the first time in the Rosenman book, long after Roosevelt died. The President wrote:

> Members of the Convention:
>
> In the century in which we live, the Democratic party has received the support of the electorate only when the party, with absolute clarity, has been the champion of progressive and liberal policies and principles of government.
>
> The party has failed consistently when through political trading and chicanery it has fallen into the control of those interests, personal and financial, which think in terms of dollars rather than in terms of human values. The Republican party has made its nominations this year at the dictation of those who, we all know, always place money ahead of human progress. The Democratic convention, as appears from the events of today, is divided on this fundamental issue. Until the Democratic party through this convention makes overwhelmingly clear its stand in favor of progress and liberalism, and shakes off all the shackles of control fastened upon it by the forces of conservatism, reaction and appeasement, it will not continue its march of victory.
>
> It is without question that certain political influences pledged to reaction in domestic affairs and to appeasement in foreign affairs have been busily engaged behind the scenes in promotion of discord since this Convention convened. Under those circumstances I cannot in all honor, and will not, merely for political expediency, go along with the cheap bargaining and political maneuvering which have brought about party dissension in this convention.
>
> It is best not to straddle ideals.
>
> In these days of danger when democracy must be more

vigilant, there can be no connivance with the kind of politics which has internally weakened nations abroad before the enemy has struck from without. It is best for America to have the fight here and now.

I wish to give the Democratic party the opportunity to make its historic decision clearly and without equivocation. The party must go wholly one way or wholly the other. I cannot face in both directions at the same time.

By declining the honor of the nomination for the Presidency, I can restore that opportunity to the Convention. I so do.

It is conceivable that Roosevelt would have declined, opening the way for the convention to renominate him and take a second vote on the Vice-Presidency—the only course the convention could choose and still think in terms of winning in November. But it is inconceivable that Roosevelt would have declined in the words he wrote in advance. His message reads like an angry man getting his anger out of his system by dictating a letter never meant to be mailed.

For there was no connection between isolationism and the opposition to Wallace. The Southern Democrats who cast their votes for Bankhead, and would have supported anybody but Wallace, had been the principal supporters in Congress of the President's internationalist, interventionist policies. As for convention opposition being reactionary, it had endorsed the New Deal without either a public or private word of dissent. As far as dissension in the convention was concerned, it had been limited to dissatisfaction with the way Presidential agents had ignored protocol.

If it was bluff, it carried the day anyhow. Those in the room with Roosevelt in Washington breathed a collective sigh of relief when the radio brought the ballot totals for the Vice-Presidency, showing that "the Boss" had had his way. The Wallace nomination came after midnight, Chicago time, and the President delivered to it, immediately thereafter, his own acceptance speech.

He gave in it his first public explanation of his thinking on the third term, saying:

> During the spring of 1939, world events made it clear to all but the blind and partisan that a great war in Europe had become not merely a possibility but a probability, and that such a war would of necessity deeply affect the future of this nation.
>
> When the conflict first broke out last September, it was still my intention to announce clearly and simply at an early date that under no circumstances would I accept re-election. This fact was well-known to my friends and I think was understood by many citizens.
>
> It soon became evident, however, that such a public statement on my part would be unwise from the point of view of sheer public duty. As President of the United States it was my clear duty, with the aid of the Congress, to preserve our neutrality, to shape our program of defense to meet rapid changes, to keep our domestic affairs adjusted to shifting world conditions and to sustain the policy of the good neighbor.
>
> It was also my obvious duty to maintain to the utmost the influence of this mighty nation in our effort to prevent the spread of war and to sustain by all legal means those governments threatened by other governments which had rejected the principles of democracy.
>
> Swift-moving foreign events made necessary swift action at home and beyond the seas. Plans for national defense had to be expanded and adjusted to meet new forms of warfare. American citizens and their property had to be safeguarded in many foreign zones of danger. National unity in the United States became a prime essential in the face of the development of unbelievable types of espionage and international treachery.
>
> Every day that passed called for the postponement of personal plans and partisan debate until the latest possible moment. The normal conditions under which I would have made public declaration of my personal desires were wholly gone. And so, thinking solely of the national good and of the

international scene, I came to the reluctant conclusion that such declaration should not be made before the national convention.

It was accordingly made to you within an hour after the announcement of the permanent organization of this convention [Barkley's election as permanent chairman]. Like any other man, I am complimented by the honor you have done me, but I know you will understand the spirit in which I say that no call of party alone would prevail on me to accept re-election to the Presidency. The real decision to be made in these circumstances is not the acceptance of a nomination but rather an ultimate willingness to serve if chosen by the electorate of the United States.

He recalled that in setting up the defense program, and mobilizing the country's industries, he had been responsible for

drafting into the service of the nation many men and women, taking them away from important private affairs, calling them suddenly from their homes and businesses. I have asked them to leave their own work and contribute their skill and experience to the cause of the nation. I, as head of their government, have asked them to do this. . . .

. . . lying awake, as I have on many nights, I have asked myself whether I have the right as Commander-in-Chief of the Army and Navy to call on men and women to serve their country, or train themselves to serve, and at the same time decline to serve my country in my personal capacity if I am called to do so by the people of my country. . . .

The right to make that call rests with the people through the American method of a free election. Only the people themselves can draft a President. If such a draft should be made upon me, I say to you in the utmost simplicity, I will, with God's help, continue to serve you with the best of my ability and the fullness of my strength.

He thanked the convention for the nomination of Henry Wallace as his running mate, and tried to heal the breach with Farley by expressing the hope that the latter would stay in as national chairman to run the campaign. He was to pursue that tack further, later, but with no success.

He also set the tenor of his campaign by noting that it would not be a campaign in the usual sense, that world and domestic crises would keep him close to his desk, but that:

> I do expect of course, during the coming months to make my usual periodic report to the country through the medium of press conferences and radio talking. I shall not have the time or inclination to engage in purely political debate, but I shall never be loath to call the attention of the nation to deliberate or unwitting falsifications of facts which are sometimes made by political candidates.

This approach left him free to campaign when and as he saw fit, without long-standing advance commitments to specific places and events, and to carry out the business of being a candidate mostly by the business of being President.

Of his domestic record, he said:

> I do not believe for a moment that we have fully answered all of the needs of human security, but we have covered much of the road. I need not catalog the milestones of seven years, for every individual and family in the land knows that the average of their personal lives has been made safer, sounder and happier than it has ever been before.
>
> I do not think they want the gains in these directions to be repealed or even placed in the charge of those who would give them mere lip service, with no heart service.

He again allied America with those opposing Hitler, saying:

> It is our credo, unshakeable to the end, that we must live under the liberties that were first heralded by the Magna Carta and placed into glorious operation through the Declaration of Independence, the Constitution of the United States and the Bill of Rights. The government of the United States for the past seven years has had the courage to oppose openly, by every peaceful means, the spread of the dictator form of government.

Then came a warning that the Republicans could become the party of appeasement, which he coupled with his own pledge that he would fight Hitler as hard in the four years ahead as he had in those preceding. He said:

> If our government should pass to other hands next January, untried hands, inexperienced hands, we can merely hope and pray that they will not substitute appeasement and compromise with those who seek to destroy all of the democracies everywhere, including here.
>
> I would not undo if I could the efforts I made to prevent war from the moment it was threatened, and to restrict the area of carnage down to the last minute. I do not now soften the condemnation expressed by Secretary Hull and myself from time to time for the acts of aggression which have wiped out ancient, liberty-loving, peace-pursuing countries. . . . I do not resent the sentiments of sympathy with all free peoples resisting such aggression or begrudge the material aid we have given them.
>
> I do not regret my consistent endeavor to awaken this country of ours to the menace for us and all we hold dear. I have pursued these efforts in the face of appeaser fifth columnists who charged me with hysteria and war-mongering, but I felt it my duty, my simple inescapable duty, to arouse my countrymen to the dangers of new forces let loose in the world.
>
> So long as I am President, I will do all I can to insure that that foreign policy remains our foreign policy. All that I have done to maintain the peace for this country and prepare it morally as well as physically for whatever contingencies may be in store, I submit to the judgment of the people.

The President, while standing on high moral grounds, was also being an astute campaigner. No matter what the platform said, no matter what Willkie said, Roosevelt had set the major issue for the campaign, earmarking the Democrats as the friends of the democracies and foes of the aggressors, and tagging the Republicans as subject to influence by the appeasers. As long as his aid to the democracies remained "all aid short of war," he was on solid political ground.

8 The Willkie Strategy

In retrospect the campaign of every winning candidate looks good. He and his managers are complimented for having won by the use of well thought-out strategy and tactics; for having taken full advantage along the campaign trail of every opportunity that developed. Things that looked like mistakes before Election Day are glossed over or forgotten. In parallel, the campaign of the loser is invariably viewed as having been ill conceived and poorly executed. This happens even when nothing the loser could have done would have changed the result—when his opponent would have had to work miracles to snatch defeat out of the jaws of victory.

In 1940, from the moment the polls closed, the votes counted and disaster was official, the Willkie campaign strategy and tactics came in for more than the usual amount of post mortem analysis, all highly critical of the candidate's decisions. Much of this stemmed from his having taken away the nomination at the convention from so many regular Republicans with continuing followings within the party organization. It was perfectly understandable for the top men—ruled out because they were deemed to have no chance themselves—to say that it had served the party right for picking an outright amateur who wasn't even a Republican. From there they moved easily into the position that if a regular Republican had been the nominee and had campaigned on a straight anti-New Deal platform, that man would have won. Parenthetically, this attack on Willkie's campaign grew rather than lessened after 1940, when it became apparent that he was a candidate for the 1944 nomination. The Taft and Dewey men wanted no second Willkie blitz.

Actually the thing that made Willkie's 1940 campaign unusual was not that it was criticized so much later for the mistakes made, but that the campaign looked so bad at the time it was being waged. It started out on a high presidential key and wound up at the alderman level, but for reasons entirely different from those given later by his disappointed convention rivals.

Willkie's problem from the start—which would also have faced any other Republican nominee that year—was to hold the party regulars and anti-New Deal Democrats while winning over enough independents to give himself a popular majority. Based on the 1936 vote of 27,750,000 for Roosevelt and 16,680,000 for Landon, he needed all the Landon voters, plus 6,000,000 of the 1936 Rooseveltites as well as an even break among the 6,000,000 new voters that, it was estimated correctly, the 1940 election would bring to the polls.

Willkie had this figured out correctly and was originally committed to making his entire campaign one of pursuit of the uncommitted, with a Billy Sunday or Billy Graham evangelistic crusade. His premise was that the Landon vote was made up of lifelong Republicans who would never leave their party, plus anti-New Deal Democrats who had already left it, and that both would vote for him or anyone else against Roosevelt, whether he courted them or not. My own spot checks after the election in 1940 uncovered no one who had voted against Roosevelt in 1936 who voted for him in the Willkie campaign.

So Willkie started out as an independent, or at least was committed to that position. But as the days, weeks and months went on, he yielded more and more to pressures that he take positions popular with the regular Republicans, so that he wound up presenting only vestiges of his original platform and personal convictions, and returning publicly to them only after his defeat. For the duration of the campaign he lost nearly all his shine as a sincere, frank-speaking political phenomenon, and thus most of the attraction for the independents who had to be wooed away from Roosevelt. The post-election claims of the organization men that he had lost because he had not courted sufficiently the party regulars was sheer nonsense. It was trying to hold them that made his campaign tactics look so bad.

The extent of Willkie's campaign compromises with his own convictions was due, in the author's judgment, to three separate things. First, having virtually stolen the nomination from under the noses of so many party professionals, he wanted to demonstrate his good will and desire to get along with everyone. Liking and being liked were inherent in Willkie. Secondly, he was a rank amateur in politics. It is typical of such that having earlier regarded the political profession with disdain, they feel their only line for future success once they are in it is to emulate or outdo the professionals at their own game of compromise and double talk. However, the true professional, brought up in the art of compromise, knows just how far he can swing away from where he started without looking like a chump. He knows what compromises can reasonably be expected from him and those which would cost him more in stature than he could hope to gain in votes. He never shows up as poorly as the overzealous amateur playing what he considers to be the "political game."

Thirdly, Willkie was inevitably surrounded on his campaign train and at campaign stops, by Republican Party pros each interested in getting out the maximum Republican vote in his own area, and whose constant advice and admonition was that he should stick to tried and true Republican principles and campaign approaches. It was difficult for him to say no to each and every aspect, and under this type of pressure, he gave and gave and gave.

His first major mistake, based on his desire to show how really easy he was to get along with, if principle were not involved, came only two hours after his nomination. He met at 3:00 A.M. in his Philadelphia hotel room with most of the top men of the Republican Party, there to congratulate the winner, patch up wounds left over from the balloting and to get from Willkie his choice for the Vice-Presidency which would be ratified by the convention that same afternoon.

Willkie had been thinking in unconventional terms about the Vice-Presidency, favoring Governor Raymond B. Baldwin of Connecticut—young, attractive and free of old machine ties or handicapping connection with the Old Deal or votes in Congress. The Baldwin selection would have rejected the traditionalist concept that the presidential and vice-presidential nominees must come from different sections of the country. It would have been the logical extension of Willkie's argument to the people that it was the man and what he stood for, not his place of birth or previous political coloration, that should count in the election ahead.

Instead, when Joe Martin suggested Charles L. McNary of Oregon, the leader of the Republican minority in the U.S. Senate, Willkie gave the McNary suggestion instantaneous approval. Martin had time for only a capsulized summary of the McNary-for-Vice-President argument; that it would balance the ticket geographically, that it would be pleasing to the members of the House and the Senate, and that it would make a strong appeal to the farm vote, when Willkie cut him off by saying:

"Call him up and tell him."

He never considered that to the voters, in accepting the balanced ticket concept, he was shedding the first skin of his independence of tradition for tradition's sake.

The McNary selection was poor for additional reasons. As Republican leader of the Senate he could be held responsible for the isolationist voting record of most of the GOP senators, as well as his own personal record, which was cast up, during the campaign, as opposed to Willkie's own thinking. The GOP Senate as well as House records negated Willkie's own beliefs and public positions on the neutrality act amendments, aid to the Allies, even domestic defense appropriations. The Senator's single posture as a liberal lay in the area of aid to the farmer. As co-author of the long-pending but never implemented McNary-Haugen program for farm aid, his name was well known to the farm population. It was also true that he had never been able to get his party to back it, even when they had the power, in the Hoover Administration, to enact it into law.

Willkie's desire to please the Republican Party professionals through the device of giving them a substantial say in the campaign machinery led to another costly selection. John Hamilton, to whom Willkie owed much for his part in the nominating procedure, wanted to be re-elected national chairman. Before the convention, Willkie with typical ebullience told Hamilton he didn't even want the nomination if Hamilton wouldn't run the campaign. But Hamilton had made many enemies.

The Taft, Dewey and even Hoover people were angry at Hamilton for having allied himself with Willkie while he was head of the party machinery, to them an act of unneutrality. Helen and Ogden Reid, owners of the internationalist *New York Herald Tribune* were bitter at Hamilton because they interpreted his comment on Henry Stimson's acceptance of the War Secretaryship under Roosevelt as "reading Stimson out of the party." Alf Landon, in control of the Kansas machinery, had even dropped Hamilton as the Kansas national committeeman. With Hamilton's head sought from so many directions, Willkie appointed a committee to come up with a solution.

Their remedy, adopted by Willkie, was to make Joe Martin the national chairman, and therefore campaign manager, while Hamilton reverted to the spot he had been in from 1934 to 1936, paid executive director. Willkie hailed the Martin choice, and as the campaign went on, was thus tied in closer and closer with Martin's outstandingly isolationist and conservative record in the House, where he, like McNary in the Senate, was the minority leader. In addition, Martin, tied up in Congress, contributed little to campaign organization work. Also he was far more parochial in his outlook than Hamilton.

Willkie's original approach to the issues had been keyed to removing isolationism versus interventionism as a major issue—by agreeing substantially with Roosevelt on what had to be done in the face of the threat to America's freedom—and concentrating on the failures the New Deal had registered in promoting its own objectives on the domestic front. His approach—the need for an expanded economy—was not substantially different from that of John F. Kennedy on the Democratic ticket twenty years later.

It was all spelled out in his acceptance speech delivered to a tremendous crowd gathered in his home town of Elwood, Indiana, on a miserably hot and humid August 17th, and the speech fell flat on its face when delivered.

He called for a crusade, with a new leadership "that believes in the destiny of America."

> The promises of the present administration cannot lead you to victory against Hitler, or against anyone else. . . . It does not preach the doctrine of growth. It preaches the doctrine of division. We are not asked to make more for ourselves. We are asked to divide among ourselves that which we already have. . . . The New Deal doctrine does not seek risk, it seeks safety. Let us call it the "I pass" doctrine. The New Deal dealt it and refused to make any more bets on the American future. . . .
>
> . . . if you start like the New Deal with the idea that we shall never have many more automobiles or radios, that we can not develop many new inventions of importance, that our standard of living must remain about what it is, the rest of the argument is easy. Since a few people have more than they need and millions have less than they need, it is necessary to redivide the wealth and turn it back from the few to the many. But this can only make the poor poorer and the

rich less rich. It does not really distribute wealth, it distributes poverty.

Picturing himself as both a true and early liberal, he decried the concentration of power in industry and finance which had existed before 1929, and endorsed each of the New Deal's stated domestic goals, saying:

> I believe that the forces of free enterprise must be regulated. I am opposed to business monopolies. I believe in collective bargaining, by representatives of labor's own free choice, without any interference and in full protection of those obvious rights. I believe in the maintenance of minimum standards for wages and maximum standards for hours. I believe such standards could constantly improve. I believe in the federal regulation of interstate utilities, of securities markets and of banking. I believe in federal pensions, in adequate old age benefits and in unemployment allowances.

He included farm parity prices, farm cooperatives and rural electrification, and his only sop to the Republicans who in their hearts still regarded such New Deal measures as heresy or treason was in his plea for greater productivity which could come only from the ending of government harassment, saying:

> American liberalism does not consist merely in reforming things. It consists also in making things. The ability to grow, the ability to make things, is the measure of man's welfare on this earth. To be free, man must be creative. . . .
>
> I say that we must substitute for the philosophy of distributed scarcity the philosophy of unlimited productivity. I stand for the restoration of full production and re-employment by private enterprise in America. And I say that we must henceforth ask certain questions of every reform and of every law to regulate business or industry. We must ask: Has it encouraged our industries to produce? Has it created new opportunities for our youth? Will it increase our standard of living? Will it encourage us to open up a new and bigger world?
>
> A reform that cannot pass these tests is not a truly liberal reform. It is an "I pass" reform. It does not tend to strengthen

our system, but to weaken it. It exposes us to aggressors, whether economic or military. It encourages class distinctions and hatreds. And it will lead us inevitably, as I believe we are now headed, toward a form of government alien to ours. . . .

It is from weakness that people reach for dictators and concentrated government power. Only the strong can be free. And only the productive can be strong.

In the foreign affairs segment of the Elwood speech, Willkie, over the objection of his Republican professional advisers, came out for the draft. He also espoused aid to England and rejected coexistence with a victorious Nazi Germany. He said:

In the foreign policy of the United States, as in its domestic policy, I would do everything to defend American democracy and I would refrain from doing anything that would injure it. We must not permit our emotions—our sympathies or hatreds—to move us from that fixed principle.

For instance we must not shirk the necessity of preparing our sons to take care of themselves in case the defense of America leads to war. . . . I cannot ask the American people to put their faith in me without recording my conviction that some form of selective service is the only democratic way in which to secure the trained and competent manpower we need for national defense.

Also, in the light of my principle, we must honestly face our relationship with Great Britain. We must admit that the loss of the British fleet would greatly weaken our defense. This is because the British fleet has for years controlled the Atlantic, leaving us free to concentrate in the Pacific. If the British fleet were lost or captured, the Atlantic might be dominated by Germany, a power hostile to our way of life, controlling in that event most of the ships and ship-building facilities of Europe.

This would be a calamity for us. We might be exposed to attack on the Atlantic. Our defense would be weakened until we could build a navy and air force strong enough to defend both coasts. Also, our foreign trade would be profoundly affected. That trade is vital to our prosperity. But if we had to deal with a Europe dominated by the present German

> trade policies, we might have to change our trade methods to some totalitarian form. This is a prospect that any lover of democracy must view with consternation. . . .
>
> The President of the United States recently said: "We will extend to the opponents of force the material resources of this nation and at the same time we will harness the use of those resources in order that we . . . may have equipment and training equal to the task of any emergency and every defense. . . ."
>
> I am in agreement with these two principles as I understand them, and I do not understand them as implying military involvement in the present hostilities. As an American citizen, I am glad to pledge my wholehearted support to the President in whatever action he may take in accordance with these principles.

In his preamble to the foreign affairs discussion, Willkie said that "no man can guarantee to maintain peace."

In his postscript to his own views, he attacked Roosevelt for having "dabbled in inflammatory statements and manufactured panics," for having

> courted a war for which the country is hopelessly unprepared and which it emphatically does not want.
>
> He has secretly meddled in the affairs of Europe and he has even unscrupulously encouraged other countries to hope for more help than we are able to give."

In his windup, he challenged the President to meet him in a series of debates on the "fundamental issues" of the campaign.

The Elwood speech was the first and last speech of the campaign not written under pressure of time, and it was the last one Willkie delivered without wandering broadly from his prepared text. He hoped that his reasoned analysis of the lack of domestic growth would hold the headlines. Not surprisingly, *The New York Times* headline—and it was typical—read:

Willkie for Draft Training,
Says President Courts War;
Challenges him to Debate.

From then on, the Willkie campaign was plagued with an atmosphere of confusion and impulsiveness, for which the candidate himself was responsible. The picture of him being able to organize the nation better for either peace or war was blurred by his own inability to organize either his campaign or his own thinking.

When he was nominated, tradition as well as the inevitability of the Democrats taking over in the political columns for the duration of their convention called for Willkie to go offstage for a while. He did go to Colorado Springs, and had he played the game correctly, he would have devoted the three weeks intervening between Philadelphia and the Elwood speech to organizing his campaign, getting into type his basic campaign speeches as well as the acceptance talk, and even devoting some time to quiet thinking.

Instead, his headquarters at the Broadmoor Hotel was in constant chaos. He had not seen the need for professional help in such things as opening and evaluating his mail—far heavier than even a President would get—or in dealing with the demands of the press. When he did assign volunteers to opening the mail, they were political neophytes to whom political names meant nothing. The classic example involved Charles D. Hilles, the courtly and able former Republican National Chairman as well as boss of New York. He wired Willkie his congratulations and offered any help he could give in the campaign ahead. Hilles received eventually a form letter thanking him and advising that "you can best help us by joining your local Willkie Club."

There were hundreds of similar incidents involving Republican or even independent bigwigs who were less understanding than the New York veteran.

Then there was the need for a press secretary to protect both the candidate and the reporters. The latter found it impossible to live or get any sleep, day or night, with Willkie's casual and uninhibited dropping of important news to any lone newsman he met in the bar or dining room or when out for a walk, with no established facilities for getting that same news to all of the rest. All of the reporters benefitted occasionally, and suffered the rest of the time. The press finally revolted, and persuaded Willkie he needed help. At their suggestion, he sent for Lamoyne A. (Lem) Jones, a former *New York Herald Tribune* reporter who up to then had acted as Tom Dewey's press officer. Dewey released Jones, and the latter stayed with Willkie for the duration.

But even Jones couldn't keep Willkie under wraps until it was time to really start campaigning. The candidate, restless, insisted on making side trips from Colorado Springs, to Denver or any place else reachable in a day. He made personal replies to attacks on him by Democratic hatchet men, instead of having those answered by Republicans or independents operating at the same level. He got needlessly and personally involved in the details of campaign financing, and the position he took didn't ring true. The new Hatch Act put a limit of three million dollars on the amount that could be spent in a national campaign, and five thousand dollars as the limit any one person could contribute. The counsel to the Republican National Committee advised the committee that the law really put a limit of three million spent or five thousand contributed to any single committee, and that the campaign needs could be met by having several committees spend the money and receive the contributions. Willkie spontaneously insisted this was an evasion of the law which he would not condone. His words sat poorly because of the elaborate nature of the advertising and headquarters setups of the Willkie movement coming into being with his approval, and which were bound to ignore his own budget limitations.

Then there was Willkie's idea that he could win by getting his message across personally to all of the voters. He jokingly told reporters that "wherever and whenever two or more Americans are gathered in my honor, I will make a speech," and then tried to live up to it. He had mapped a very ambitious opening campaign tour, which would take him through Indiana,

Illinois, Iowa, Missouri, Kansas, Oklahoma, Texas, New Mexico, Arizona, California, Washington, Idaho, Montana, North and South Dakota, Wisconsin and Michigan. The first major speech was scheduled for Coffeyville, Kansas, where Willkie had once taught school.

But at the very start of that trip, on his way to Coffeyville, he made full speeches from the back of his railroad train—this was before airplane travel became routine—at Joliet, Morris, Ottawa, La Salle, Peoria, Galesburg and Rock Island. By nightfall of the second day, his voice had given out, and the campaign train was that of a literally speechless candidate.

At the very start his off-the-cuff oratory was marked by two fluffs. While touring Chicago and its suburbs, he made a reference to "here in Chicago." Told by the crowd he was not in Chicago, but in Cicero, he proclaimed: "Okay, the hell with Chicago," which was the banner quotation in the Chicago papers that day.

And at Joliet he had let fly at the Roosevelt Administration's foreign policy so loosely that Jones had to issue a statement explaining that the candidate had "mis-spoken himself." More on this later.

The thirteen-car campaign train carried a record number of correspondents covering a presidential pretender, but its most amazing feature was the car assigned to Willkie's speechwriters. The car was aptly nicknamed the "squirrel cage."

It carried a capable team of writers, headed by Russell Davenport, who were supposed to bat out speeches that the candidate would absorb and use as a base for his extemporaneous remarks. The writers had virtually no time to discuss the content with the nominee, who could and did use up speeches far faster than they could prepare them. Willkie frequently let the tone of the crowd determine what he said and how he said it, regardless of script.

Even if he did adhere to one speech and one theme for a day, he improved the speech as he delivered it, so that often, by midnight, it was a first-class address. But it was the early version for the day which got into newspaper type and stayed unchanged, because Willkie altered only the words, not the theme, and there was a practical limit to the word changes the reporters could wire.

His voice eventually was restored by the ministrations of a throat specialist flown to the campaign train from New York, but for the rest of the time right up to Election Day, there was a hoarseness in his delivery and a constant uncertainty whether or not he would be able to meet the demands he himself had set.

Willkie never abandoned the domestic economy argument of his Elwood speech, particularly the refrain that "only the productive can be strong, and only the strong can be free." And he kept his finale, a plea, with his arms outstretched to the crowd to "join me, join me in this great crusade."

But under pressure from Republican advisers, and in response to crowd reaction, he adopted as his main issues the danger of Roosevelt leading the nation into war, plus challenging the credibility of anything the President said to the contrary.

In direct contradiction of his own Elwood declaration that no one man, and no one nation, could guarantee the continuance of peace, he stressed more and more that his own election would lessen the danger of America's entry into the war. While continuing to approve the draft, he nevertheless raised more often the prospect that if he were defeated, the men about to go into training would soon be fighting.

For example, when he recalled Roosevelt's 1932 campaign pledge to cut federal expenses by 25 per cent, Willkie said:

"If Roosevelt's word is no better now than it was then, you can count on our men being on transports for Europe six months from now." The headlines read: "Willkie sees us at war by April 1." This was the statement that particularly led to his admission, when he testified at a congressional hearing on the Lend-Lease legislation early in 1941, that he had indulged in some "campaign oratory."

Willkie, irritated by the charge that all Republicans were isolationists, tried to show that Roosevelt himself had been the nation's leading isolationist. He linked together Roosevelt's sabotaging the London Economic Conference of 1933, signing the neutrality law of 1935, and urging a conference settlement of the issues at Munich in 1938 as proof that Roosevelt had never really taken an early or firm stand against Hitler. Willkie nullified the soundness of this argument—and it did possess merit—when at Joliet he expanded it to say:

"Roosevelt telephoned Mussolini and Hitler and urged them to sell Czecho-Slovakia down the river at Munich." This is what produced Jones' acknowledgement that the candidate had "misspoken himself."

Willkie constantly attacked the Roosevelt Administration for having failed to end unemployment and for having failed to step up defense production—both arguments that had less validity when made than they would have had a year earlier. Everywhere people were getting jobs, and everywhere there were signs of defense industries that had never existed before.

Willkie's Elwood speech had stressed the danger of totalitarianism getting a foothold in America as a result of the "planned economy" approach of the New Deal. Under the campaign pressures, he more and more linked the danger of totalitarianism with the third-term issue, so that he wound up predicting that if Roosevelt were elected for a third term, totalitarianism would come within the four years of that term—that the 1940 election was the last free election the nation would ever see. If this had any effect, it was to call attention to the fact that Roosevelt, unlike any dictator, was running for continuation in office by the free election process.

He made still another miscalculation in the field of foreign affairs. Roosevelt had been privately negotiating with Winston Churchill, who had been pleading for the immediate transfer of fifty American destroyers, relics of World War I, which England could use to protect her sea lanes from the German submarines. The deal, agreed upon, called for England to transfer, by gift or lease, a number of bases in the Caribbean that the United States could use to protect the Panama Canal and other approaches from the south.

The arrangement fell completely within the scope of Willkie's own foreign policy as defined in the Elwood speech, and when Roosevelt sent emissaries to Willkie to tell him what went on and solicit his approval, Willkie could have given it. Instead, he regarded Roosevelt's confidence as an attempt to tie him in with the Roosevelt policies. Even when the deal was announced and was hailed by all of the interventionists and most of the isolationists as good for America's defense, Willkie declined to endorse it. Some of the isolationists called it an act of war on Germany. Willkie called it the "most dictatorial act of any President in the whole history of the United States," basing his criticism on the fact that Roosevelt had made the transfer by executive order, rather than by act of Congress.

While his stand on the draft was definite and clear, even to the point of opposing a Republican amendment which would have deferred registration until after Election Day—he proceeded to muddy the legislative waters by violently phrased opposition to an amendment that gave the government the power, if needed, to seize any industrial plant that would not cooperate in the war effort. The amendment had really been written into the law to appease those who were arguing that if labor was subject to conscription, so should capital be. Willkie unexplainably denounced it as an attempt to "Sovietize" American industry. Even the Republican isolationists in Congress who had accepted the amendment without demurrer were embarrassed by Willkie's outburst.

Willkie devoted the last five weeks of his campaign to the states east of the Mississippi and north of the Ohio—the big industrial or farm and industry states with the electoral votes he would need to win. And in them he raised more vigorously than ever the issue of the war and of Roosevelt's credibility.

He made statements like:

"Is there anybody here who really thinks the President is sincerely trying to keep us out of war?"

Another was: "I want to know if there are any secret commitments, international understandings to put us into the war, that the President hasn't told the people about."

Willkie drew good crowds everywhere, great crowds in the big cities. But it was apparent throughout that not all who turned out to see him were going to vote for him, or were even willing to be persuaded. In the center of town, Chicago's Loop or New York's Broadway, the streets would be jammed with Willkie enthusiasts, including many young people casting their votes with enthusiasm for the new man on the political scene. A quarter-century later there were still men and women who cut their political eye teeth as members of the Willkie Clubs who remembered their youthful enthusiasm.

But on the outskirts of town, in front of the local stockyards or mill or manufacturing plant, the workmen on their lunch hours were interested in the Willkie caravan and in seeing the man himself, but there was little cheering. Eventually, as Willkie continued his attacks on the President, the coldness manifested itself in hostility. A few people got around to throwing things at or in the general direction of the candidate. While such incidents were unorganized, they happened often enough to warrant a *New York Times* box score of vegetables thrown and hits registered.

The first incident was early, in Inglewood, California, when a tomato missed the candidate but spattered other members of his party. It got more serious later on. In a tour of Detroit, a cantaloupe was heaved from a hotel window, and in quick succession came a chair, a telephone book, a wastebasket and a heavy ash tray. On way by rail to Kalamazoo, a stone went through the window of the dining car, and flying glass cut a newspaper correspondent eating dinner. In Pontiac, three eggs were thrown, and one splashed Mrs. Willkie, causing the candidate for once to lose his temper. He himself was hit by a potato in Boston, while a stone, a tomato and a light bulb scored near misses on that same New England swing. In Rome, New York, he was hit by a tomato and on his last swing through Chicago, by an egg.

The incidents reflected the failure of Willkie, in his big city speeches, to make a dent in the hostility of labor at the time to the Republican Party, no matter who headed it and no matter how hard Willkie tried to court it. His efforts, of course, were limited by his commitment to the party that nominated him. Unions, particularly the industrial unions of the still-new CIO, were the bête noire of industry and of the basic Republican voter, who opposed Roosevelt's New Deal as an American manifestation of the labor governments which occasionally ruled France or England.

Despite his Elwood speech, which endorsed nearly all of the domestic ventures of the New Deal, Willkie could never commit himself to more of the same. All he could do rationally was to expound his theory of an expanded economy—if governmental restrictions were removed—that would bring more and better jobs. Since he could not endorse specifically the operations under the Wagner Labor Relations Act, the labor speeches he delivered could be and usually were cut to ribbons by the local labor leaders the following day.

In Pittsburgh he promised if elected to appoint as Secretary of Labor a leader of organized labor. He unfortunately ad-libbed—"and it won't be a woman either." This won him no additional labor support and very likely affronted active feminists, who regarded Roosevelt's appointment of Frances Perkins of his Cabinet as a milestone.

His last desperate venture was to court the support of the redoubtable John L. Lewis, the sulking lion of the labor movement. Lewis, then the perpetual head of the United Mine Workers and the President of the CIO, had supported Roosevelt with all his might and money in 1936. He then had broken with the President, presumably because Roosevelt failed to recognize him as the only spokesman for labor in the nation. Early in 1940, Lewis backed Burton K. Wheeler for the presidential nomination and predicted Roosevelt couldn't possibly be elected for a third term.

Willkie managed to meet secretly with Lewis. What commitments the candidate made were never disclosed, but Lewis immediately bought his own radio time and on a Friday night, eleven days before election, spent half an hour on the air in a nationwide broadcast, carried by all networks. He demanded Roosevelt's defeat and pledged his own resignation as president of the CIO if Roosevelt was re-elected. The beetle-browed labor boss had an immense listening audience that night as he spewed out invective.

In effect, Lewis told the millions of CIO men and women that they had to choose at the polls between having Lewis as president of the CIO or Roosevelt as President of the U.S.A. Labor was happy with Roosevelt as President of the United States, and while they were happy with Lewis as CIO head, their reaction was that there was no reason for Lewis to pose the choice. It probably stiffened the determination of the rival American Federation of Labor leaders to outdo themselves in Roosevelt's behalf.

The sum total, so near the end of the campaign, was a letdown. One story, probably apochryphal, is that the Lewis speech was heard by a high-ranking Republican fund raiser sitting around the room with a group of well-heeled businessmen from whom he was about to seek contributions. When Lewis finished, the fund raiser said:

"Well, gentlemen, you now know the desperateness of the Republican Party position."

One reason the author does not take the story at face value—though vouched for by usually reliable sources—is that money had poured in—from big business, stockbrokers, industrialists, well-endowed families—to finance the most lavish campaign setups all over the nation. Much was wasted—there were seventeen separate Willkie headquarters on Manhattan Island alone—but still there was a surplus when it all was over. What the campaign lacked was not money, but coherence.

9 The Roosevelt Strategy

Roosevelt's strategy was simplicity itself—to spend as much time as possible appearing as the President of the United States and as little as possible as a political candidate. He began building the foundation for this position, brick by brick, in the summer of 1939, a full year before the Democratic nominating convention.

In private long before he made it publicly, he made the point that he did not want to run, would in no sense seek the nomination. Then, yielding to the self-created convention draft, he was able to campaign as he wanted to.

Both he and Mrs. Roosevelt—the latter without any coaching from her husband—told the Chicago convention that the President would be too busy with affairs of state to make the usual type of campaign. Until the last few weeks before election, his carefully selected position was that he was a busy chief executive serving his country in time of great need who could not and would not find time to spend in the political arena.

And Roosevelt *was* busy with the problems of the nation. He was supervising, in his typically formless, indefinable way, the creation of the new and tremendous defense industry that was eventually to produce incredible numbers of planes, fighting ships, carriers, submarines, landing craft, freighters, tanks, artillery, machine guns and rifles for the United States and Britain and later the Russians and Free French when they became allied in the battle against Hitler.

He was also busy directing the foreign policy of the nation along one line—doing anything possible to stop Hitler. He was as well creating a great set of armed forces to back up that foreign policy no matter where it led. And he was emerging as the world spokesman for democracy in opposition to those who saw it bound to be supplanted by either Fascism or Communism as the great force of the world.

Roosevelt kept busy on the home front too, guiding the thinking of the American people along interventionist lines while trying to maintain peace between capital and labor in the increasingly lucrative defense production effort. Many of the things that took up his time were public, many were private. All involved action sooner or later.

It is an axiom of politics that the incumbent office-holder, anyplace from bottom to top of the governmental structure, enjoys a tremendous election advantage over his opponent if he has any kind of performance record behind him. The advantage held by the President of the United States in 1940 was described by Turner Catledge, brilliant Washington correspondent, in these words:

"Mr. Roosevelt can act while Mr. Willkie can only talk, and talk for the most part about the President's acts."

No President has ever used the campaign tools that were his by virtue of his office more effectively than did Roosevelt in his third-term venture. In many ways, he controlled both events and the timing of events. He used both to bolster his stature and prestige with an electorate much concerned about the fate of America and the world.

And while he operated at the high policy level, he saw to it that his aides and underlings ran a well-organized hit-and-run guerrilla campaign at the political level.

Roosevelt really opened his campaign with the Stimson-Knox

appointments to his Cabinet, even before the GOP had selected its own presidential nominee. The move was a typically Roosevelt mixture of good government and good politics. He did need stronger men than he had in the War and Navy departments, in view of the vast expansion of both that was certain to come. The Republicans he selected were better than their Democratic predecessors. He could have selected better Democrats. But by selecting from the other party, he gave a national rather than a party flavor to the whole drive for a new and real Army and Navy. He had decided on the move at least six months earlier. By timing it on the eve of the Republican convention, he created the most disorder and confusion in the Republican ranks.

When the conventions were over, in support of his fixed position that he was too busy saving the nation to campaign for office, Roosevelt scheduled only half a dozen major "political speeches." One was in mid-September, the balance in the two weeks before Election Day. But in the course of doing his job as President, he managed to be out on the stump for a full six months before the voting. This involved the making of "nonpolitical" speeches and tours and appearances.

He inspected Navy yards and new defense installations rolling out their first tanks or cannon or airplanes, and witnessed the maneuvers of the small professional Army that was to furnish the leadership and cadres for the immense force to come. No one could question the President's right or duty to have a first-hand look at what was going on. No one could question the fact that a Presidential visit or inspection bolstered the morale of the infantrymen wallowing in the mud or the factory workers putting in overtime. And no one has ever questioned that these trips were also campaign trips that benefitted his candidacy.

Every time he inspected a Navy shipyard or a tank arsenal, Administration spokesmen in the War and Navy departments had the opportunity to get the progress that was being made in defense work into the record and to the public through the press. Since the nation had had no defense industry, every bit of production was a new milestone. Even if only groundbreaking was the excuse for the visit, the eventual production capacity of the plant involved became an official figure used to give the lie to Republican claims of an Administration default in the vital national defense field.

The Roosevelt trips from Washington or Hyde Park to the hinterlands also gave the Democratic Party organizations and the labor unions the opportunity to turn out the people to greet the President, to whip up enthusiasm, to engender the early emotional or mental commitment that translates itself into votes on Election Day.

The President did not restrict his trips away from Washington to items in the defense field. Traditionally every President is invited to gatherings of a nonpolitical nature at which he is expected to speak on some subject of particular interest to the audience and suited to the occasion in terms of government action, or plans or leadership in the field. Roosevelt had always used these opportunities to the fullest advantage, and continued to do so in the 1940 campaign.

Sam Rosenman, in *Working with Roosevelt,* described Roosevelt's technique as follows:

> The President was very adept at using non-political speeches—especially during his campaigns—to derive great political benefit. He frequently used a phrase he had coined in Albany [when Governor] and about which Missy and Grace [his secretaries Marguerite LeHand and Grace Tully] and I liked to tease him.
>
> He would say innocently in prefacing a speech that he was going to talk "government, not politics" and then make what was in effect a fine political speech. It would not be in terms of political parties at all; rather it would contain generalities about government that would provide kudos for his own party and imply censure of the Republican party.
>
> After he had delivered one of these "non-political" speeches, Missy or Grace would smile guilelessly and say:

"That speech certainly was about government, not politics." This always drew a pleased laugh from the President, followed by a mock-indignant protestation of innocence and a vehement denial that he had intended any politics at all.

A classic example of Roosevelt using a nonpolitical speech to discuss principles of government was his September 20, 1940, speech at the University of Pennsylvania. His subject was the spirit of democracy and what had to be done to preserve it. Willkie had been charging that Roosevelt's third-term candidacy spelled dictatorship and the end of free elections. Roosevelt, without mentioning Willkie or his charge, hailed the American system of free elections and recalled that no dictator had ever dared submit his power to the test of a vote of free people.

Such speeches kept Roosevelt in the position of the Great White Father discussing eternal truths with his people, at the same time making the effective point that a free election was being held while the atheists or agnostics on the opposition were saying it couldn't happen.

In his acceptance speech to the Chicago convention, as he disclaimed any intention of waging a political campaign, he reserved for himself the privilege of correcting any "deliberate or unwitting falsifications of fact" by the opposition in the months ahead.

In operation, this opened the door for the President to deliver at the proper time a series of derisory attacks on the Republican promises as contrasted with the Republican record and to dwell on his own record in the fields of national defense and social welfare. He waited for the very end of the campaign to do this, for three tactical reasons.

First, the longer he waited the longer he could maintain his position as the President who was too busy to indulge in politics. Second, the passage of additional time could only accentuate the differences on foreign affairs which split the Republican Party and its candidate, as evidenced by Republican votes in Congress. And finally, each month would bring into being more proof, in the form of defense statistics and employment increases, that the Administration in power was doing its job of protecting the American people from dangers abroad while increasing wages and income at home.

The split in the Republican Party became a major target of the Administration forces. Both the Democratic and Republican party platforms were alike in pledging the speedy buildup of our own defenses, the giving of aid to the enemies of aggressive, dictator-led nations, and keeping America out of the war. In the votes of Congress that followed the conventions, a majority of the Republicans in both houses voted against selective service, even after their presidential nominee had endorsed the draft as the only democratic way of getting an army big enough to protect ourselves. When Hamilton Fish, the leading congressional isolationist, proposed putting the draft off for two more months so that it would follow Election Day, most of the Republicans in Congress supported the Fish amendment against the advice of Willkie. In addition, most of the Congress Republicans had poor voting records on defense appropriations back in 1938 and 1939, when the issue first arose.

As Willkie campaigned and campaigned, a number of the Democratic leaders grew nervous, and the White House was bombarded with messages and advice, all to the effect that "if the Boss wants to win this election, he'd better get out on the stump." When Roosevelt did start campaigning as a candidate, those who gave the advice credited themselves with his having done so.

This is highly unlikely, and there is nothing in the record to show that Roosevelt ever contemplated sitting out the month of October in Hyde Park or the White House. It was against his nature. As he said during the campaign: "I'm an old campaigner, and I like a good fight."

He waited until he thought the time was ripe, and took to the stump in the key Eastern states that were the battleground and that contained the electoral votes which, added to those of the South, would assure an electoral majority.

Roosevelt held most of his fire until ten days before election, after the manpower of the nation had registered under the new Selective Service Law and had a personal stake in the defense effort. Then, in his major New York City address at Madison Square Garden, he contrasted the obstructionist votes of the Republicans in Congress with the promises of their candidate and their criticism of the Democrats for not having done more. He picked as samples the votes of Joe Martin, the House Minority leader who was Willkie's campaign manager; Bruce Barton, wealthy New York Congressman who was Willkie's choice for United States Senator from New York; and Fish, who through seniority was the ranking minority member of the House Military Affairs Committee.

His recital of the names of "Martin, Barton and Fish" in solemn cadence turned what could have been a dull analysis of votes in Congress into a popular chant of derision, used to heckle and embarrass the GOP for the balance of the campaign.

In his Boston speech that followed, he was able to call off to the people of America the cities where defense output was concentrated, to remind everyone that the Boeing and Douglas airplane plants in California were producing planes at a rate never rivalled, that ships were coming off the production lines at Camden, Fall River and elsewhere, that tanks were clanking out to testing grounds all over the country. Roosevelt destroyed much of the effectiveness of the Republican claim that most of the defense production was still to come by pinpointing the increases in production that nobody could deny.

He chose his final campaign speech, at Cleveland, to steal Willkie's theme of an expanded economy for America, and he was in a better position than Willkie to press it home because he—rather than the Republicans—had been responsible for the social progress made since 1932.

At Cleveland he said:

> I see an America where factory workers are not discarded after they reach their prime, where there is no endless chain of poverty from generation to generation. . . .

> I see an America whose rivers and valleys and lakes—hills and streams and plains—the mountains over our land and nature's wealth deep under the earth—are protected as the rightful heritage of all of the people.
>
> I see an America where small business really has a chance to flourish and grow.
>
> I see an America of great cultural and educational opportunity for all its people.
>
> I see an America where income from the land shall be implemented and protected by a government determined to guarantee to those who hoe it a fair share in the national income.
>
> I see an America where the wheels of trade and private industry continue to turn to make the goods for America; where no businessman can be stifled by the harsh hand of monopoly, and where the legitimate profits of legitimate industry are the fair reward of every businessman—big and little—in all the nation.
>
> I see an America with peace in the ranks of labor.
>
> An America where the workers are really free and—through their great unions—undominated by any outside force or by any dictator within—can take their proper place at the council table with the owners and managers of business. . . .
>
> An America where those who have reached the evening of life shall live out their years in peace and security; where pensions and insurance for these aged shall be given as a matter of right to those who through a long life of labor have served their families and their nation as well. . . .

The Cleveland speech demonstrated as well as any other that as long as he had his strength—and there was no diminution of it or concern about his health in the 1940 campaign—he was the master of any speech he delivered, of any crowd he addressed. His recitation of the domestic accomplishments and goals of the New Deal won him the wildest of applause. Roosevelt never resorted to any oratorical tricks that were obvious. He always gave the appearance of calmly seeking the audience's understanding, which in turn would bring approval.

What could have been a string of platitudes if phrased or delivered just slightly differently, he could turn into a simple yet effective program of national purpose.

His phrase-making got him into trouble only twice, and in both cases he spoke deliberately. Unlike Willkie's alfresco approach, every word Roosevelt uttered was considered in advance. He had a team of speechwriters—which for the 1940 campaign consisted of Sam Rosenman, Harry Hopkins and playwright Robert Sherwood—who worked closely with the President on every speech. He told them what ground he wanted covered, they knew his style and delivery, and yet they had to produce countless drafts to get his approval. Even in the final draft, the President made his own insertions, usually the phrases or point that made the speech memorable. He worked so much himself on the revisions that he knew the speech by heart when it came to delivering it. He could thus speak with only an occasional glance at his text, mostly to check his own penciled marks of emphasis.

In his Charlottesville speech the day Mussolini declared war on a France whose armies Hitler had already defeated, Roosevelt inserted during his delivery the words:

"And on this 10th day of June, 1940, the hand that held the dagger has struck it into the back of its neighbor."

The words had been in the original text, and Roosevelt took them out of it at the insistence of his friend, Sumner Welles, of the State Department.

Even as he uttered them, he must have known that they would rankle with many American Italians as a reflection on the national character, but he was bitter at Mussolini and anxious to arouse America to the danger of all of the dictatorships, not only Hitler's.

The second instance of a phrase plaguing him later involved its omission, not its insertion. Roosevelt, up to his Boston speech the last week of the campaign, had been pledging that "your boys are not going to be sent into any foreign wars except in case of attack." He had personally appended the last five words to a similar pledge in the party platform. When it came to including them in the Boston speech, the President, according to Rosenman, said testily:

"It's not necessary. It's implied clearly. If we are attacked it is no longer a foreign war."

That interpretation was as justified when Roosevelt added the words to the party platform as when he omitted them from the Boston speech. The omission probably reflected two political factors: the need for further assurance to the fathers and mothers of youths of draft age, and an extra concession to the Boston Irish, many of whom had little warmth toward the prospect of America fighting to save England. The Roosevelt testiness might have reflected Roosevelt's annoyance at having to make a pledge he was not so certain he could keep.

Roosevelt's high-level campaign strategy was less than successful in his selection of—and insistence on—Henry Wallace as his running mate for Vice-President. Wallace, although Secretary of Agriculture, demonstrated no particular strength in the farm belt that the President did not already possess. As a symbol of Democratic commitment to perpetuation of the New Deal, several others, Speaker Bankhead, Scott Lucas of Illinois, or even "Honest Harold" Ickes, would have done equally well.

Wallace's personal mysticism threatened the Democrats with serious embarrassment. There were a series of letters, supposedly written by Wallace to the guru, or leader, of a mystic cult, using terms and espousing theories foreign to 99 per cent of the American voters, which could have been used to ridicule Wallace. They were given or sold to the Republican National Committee, and their existence became widely known in political circles. It worried the Democratic high command, but the Republicans never published them, presumably because of lack of proof of their authenticity.

Wallace nevertheless did a good deal of the in-fighting of the campaign, carrying out the low-level attacks on the Republicans and their candidate that strategy dictated be not made by the President himself because it would be beneath his dignity.

Harold L. Ickes, the acidulous phrasemaker of the Cabinet, ridiculed Willkie's resumption for the campaign of an Indiana background, referring to him as "that simple, barefoot Wall Street lawyer." Fiorello La Guardia, New York's Mayor—who had been elected as a Republican but never supported a GOP state or national ticket as long as he lived—made countless speeches calling Willkie a front for the power trust, including a last-minute speech linking Willkie's secretary with the public utility lobby.

Ed Flynn reluctantly and embarrassedly took on the job of keeping Willkie engaged in constant conflict with the lower echelons of the Democrats. Flynn had come into the picture as Democratic National Chairman after the combined efforts of the President and his wife failed to budge Farley from his decision to resign both as national chairman and Postmaster General.

Flynn also tried and failed. Finally the President and Flynn, who were social intimates the way Roosevelt and Farley had never been, agreed that Farley's successor had to be another Irish-Catholic. When Roosevelt suggested that Flynn was the logical man, the latter could not say no. He was diffident, not the good mixer that Farley was with other politicians and the press, and he hated routine. But he was an Irish-Catholic and was known to enjoy the President's confidence. So much as he hated it, he took on the chore of holding daily press conferences in the campaign headquarters in New York's Hotel Biltmore, and fed out the daily attacks on Willkie that were prepared by the public-relations staff.

When Willkie attacked Roosevelt as the candidate of the bosses, it was Flynn who replied that Willkie's position was "just plain silly, because he himself was a member of Tammany Hall." When Willkie took time out to pooh-pooh his Tammany Hall connections—which in fact consisted of a window-dressing membership in the Democratic Club near Willkie's Park

Avenue apartment—it was Flynn who produced and distributed to the press Willkie's certificate of membership in the New York County Democratic Committee, the official name of traditionally disreputable Tammany.

The Flynn headquarters sponsored an attack on Willkie's position on the Negro question, pointing out that Elwood, longtime home of the Willkie family, had maintained a Jim Crow system of segregation without ever a word of protest from a Willkie, Wendell or otherwise. Willkie could only reply noting how long he had been out of Elwood and reaffirming his hatred of bigotry.

Joe Guffey, pro-labor Senator from Pennsylvania, was one of a number of New Deal spokesmen who used the slogan that "a vote for Willkie is a vote for Wall Street." The stock market crash of 1929 and the long depression that followed were still too fresh in the minds of the people for "Wall Street" to be anything but an epithet. Congressmen, senators, cabinet officers kept up, through the Flynn headquarters, a constant drumfire designed to keep Willkie on the defensive.

Flynn, though nominally in charge of the entire campaign setup, left the job of getting out the vote to others, and for the first time in many years, the Democrats really equipped themselves to see that every possible Roosevelt vote got to the polling place. They did this even though their big-city organizations, while high in prestige, had been losing their organizational manpower for a long time. They lacked the ability to conduct the house to house canvass in every precinct and ward that once had been their stock in trade. While never admitting it publicly, they turned to the labor unions for the manpower that they lacked. In cities such as Chicago, Detroit and Pittsburgh, the local Democratic machines enlisted the new and vigorous CIO industrial unions. The union shop stewards checked off the voting registration with the union dues, and then rounded up their members on Election Day to make sure they voted. Kelly, in Chicago, actually drew his canvassers out of the labor wards—letting the CIO men take over—and put his own people to work elsewhere, in places he would otherwise have been shorthanded.

In New York, where there was rivalry in local elections between the Democrats and those labor unions enlisted in the American Labor Party, La Guardia patched up a truce and both organizations worked side by side, closer than ever before or again, to bring the victory in which each had so much at stake.

Probably the most effective low-level attack on the Willkie campaign was the joint effort of Wallace, Flynn and New York's Governor Herbert H. Lehman.

Wallace, in a speech August 29th accepting the vice-presidential nomination, brought into the campaign the issue of Adolf Hitler, up to then as much the target of Willkie's attacks as those of the Democrats. Wallace said that while he did not want to imply the Republicans were giving aid and comfort to Hitler, everyone knew how Hitler would rejoice in a Roosevelt defeat.

When Willkie and the Republicans denounced the charge as atrocious and divisive, Flynn backed up Wallace, saying he knew Willkie could answer for himself, but not "for the many who exist solely on promoting racial and religious prejudice. Mr. Willkie can repudiate their support—as he has in one case—from now to Doomsday, but the fact still remains that these fellow travellers still support him by disseminating the vilest sort of anti-Roosevelt propaganda."

Flynn thus laid in the lap of the Republicans the activities of the American Christian Mobilization, William Dudley Pelley's Silver Shirts, Father Coughlin's Social Justice movement (which was the one Willkie had repudiated by name) the Ku Klux Klan and the German-American Bund, all of which had totalitarian and anti-Semitic aspects and were all campaigning for Roosevelt's defeat. The American Communists differed slightly in that they were not at that time tinged with anti-Semitism and had a nominal candidate of their own, but were just as active in attacking Roosevelt.

Next came Lehman, the leading Jewish officeholder in the United States, who told the New York Democratic State Convention that "nothing that could happen in the United States could give Hitler, Mussolini, Stalin and the government of Japan more satisfaction than the defeat . . . of Franklin D. Roosevelt."

Lehman's statement was completely accurate, on the basis of the relationship at the time between the heads of Germany, Italy, Russia and Japan and the head of the American government. An equally accurate statement would have been that nothing would please Winston Churchill more than the re-election of Roosevelt. Roosevelt was a tried and true enemy of the first group and friend of England, while Willkie, the newcomer, could be evaluated only on the basis of his campaign statements. On the basis of Willkie's post-election actions, he would have won, had he been elected, the same foreign enemies and friends.

Finally Wallace, on the Thursday night before election, spelled the attack out in its final form. Speaking in New York, where German-American Bund activities had led to frequent riot calls, Wallace said:

"Millions of Americans know from personal observation the extent of Nazi propaganda and Nazi performance for the election of the Republican candidate. Regimented Nazi organizations are marching in the Republican parade."

So the issue was "a vote for Willkie is a vote for Hitler."

Unfair as it was when so oversimplified, it nevertheless was implanted in the minds of many, particularly among the Jews, the Poles, the Czechs, the Norwegians and Danes, all of the races and nationalities that had suffered the most from Hitler's cruelties and aggression. It settled among them, as well as among others who hated Hitler in the name of humanity at large, the direction of the vote that had to be cast.

10 The Sound and Fury

The 1940 campaign was one of the noisiest, busiest, ever-present contest on record. It was the era in which the street-corner sound truck came into its own. These effective instruments of torture blared forth Democratic, Republican, Communist, Fascist, interventionist and isolationist gospel in urban areas throughout the nation, as far into the night as local law allowed.

It was also the era in which television had been invented but not developed, so that those who wanted both to hear and see the nominees for President had to get out of their living-room chairs and fight their way in to a meeting hall or public square. Going to a public meeting was still an event. Many paraded with banners to the scene and back again, proud of themselves, even if they cast a pale shadow compared to the torchlight parades of a still-earlier period. For Wendell Willkie's final campaign meeting, in New York's Madison Square Garden, capacity 23,000, there was a crowd of more than 50,000 lined up around the building early in the day, chanting "We Want Willkie" to keep themselves warm while waiting for the doors to open.

Roosevelt drew crowds that were even more impressive. His final swing that same week end, which took him through the five boroughs of New York City and then on up through New England, was in the nature of a triumphal tour. Literally millions lined the well-publicized travel route to cheer him on to victory.

There seemed to be more young people, more old people, more rich people, more poor people, just more people interested than ever before in personal participation in the election hoopla. The suburbs around the big cities were prime Willkie territory, and the younger members of upper-income families, having no one at home to convert, invaded the center cities to give out Willkie buttons. In Manhattan, pretty girls in neatly tailored blue uniforms teamed up as The Willkiettes and trod the sidewalks of Fifth Avenue and other main streets, advertising the Willkie candidacy. Even the buttons were bigger. I recall one ardent Roosevelt supporter who in 1932 had become the proud possessor of the largest Roosevelt button extant, about two and a half inches in diameter. She put it aside for 1936, and then again for 1940. But by that time it was outshone and outsized by the newer, bigger models.

Just as the upper-income groups paraded for Willkie, blue-collar union workers demonstrated for Roosevelt. Organized labor in 1940 was enjoying the full flavor of new-found power. Its magna carta, the Wagner National Labor Relations Act, had been upheld by the Supreme Court only as recently as 1937, and later statutes, aimed at curtailing political activity by organized labor, were years off. Every union headquarters was in effect a Roosevelt campaign headquarters, and the union men and union banners were prominent at every meeting.

Even those who just sat home and took their politics by listening to the radio got a fuller measure than before. As early as 1928 the radio had become a major vehicle for bringing the full speeches of the candidates to the voters, and use of the device increased in 1932 and 1936. And the 1940 campaign brought forth on the radio not only the voices of the presidential candidates, but also the voices and opinions of other big names, celebrities in a dozen other fields.

Claire Booth Luce fought with Dorothy Thompson for the minds of those who would listen to them as representative woman journalists; Mary Pickford and Ginger Rogers matched prestige with Helen Hayes and Helen Gahagan Douglas; Joe Louis with Jack Dempsey. On opposite sides, and usually on different programs, they and countless others helped saturate the air waves with politics.

The candidates, their managers and their press agents fought hard for free space in the news columns, and on the basis of newspaper adage that names make news, they got plenty of coverage. But the output was so immense that, for the portion of the campaign I spent in the news room of my own paper, *The New York Times,* I had to arm myself nightly with two wastebaskets, rather than the usual one, to dispose of the material sent in which was not "fit to print."

While theoretically Franklin D. Roosevelt was too busy with affairs of office to campaign until late October, the Democratic drive against Willkie started the day the latter was nominated. A good deal of it was devoted to ridicule. Democratic spokesmen called the Willkie nomination "the charge of the electric light brigade"; New York's Mayor, Fiorello La Guardia, an ex-Republican, said that he preferred "Roosevelt with his known faults to Willkie with his unknown virtues."

The Republicans, in turn, tried to heap scorn on Roosevelt and all his tribe. They picked up a Wallace description of Roosevelt as the "indispensable man" and hurled it as a sarcastic epithet at the President. The fact that all three Roosevelt sons of fighting age were in or on the way into the armed forces with commissions was held against the President. This, it was believed, would be resented by the families of all those who went in as privates.

Both sides maneuvered for big names. For example, Charles A. Lindbergh, the aviator who had once been the unchallenged idol of America, addressed forty thousand people at Soldiers Field in Chicago, under the auspices of the Citizens Committee to keep America out of war. He urged cooperation with Germany if it turned out the winner in Europe. The same night General John J. Pershing, World War I Commander of the AEF, was brought out of retirement to make a radio speech asking all-out aid to Britain, including the transfer or sale to her of at least fifty of the three hundred World War I destroyers that had been in mothballs since 1918.

Lindbergh did not urge the election of Willkie, nor did Pershing ask a vote for Roosevelt, but the effect was the same as if they had.

The issue of transferring our surplus destroyers to Britain was the first of two war-connected items on which the opposing presidential candidates took positions.

The German submarines were sinking so much food and matériel headed for the British Isles that Britain was in danger of being starved out of the war. The Royal Navy was spread too thin to protect the ships in convoy. Winston Churchill told Franklin Roosevelt, in the course of the private correspondence they conducted, that England needed American destroyers desperately. Roosevelt agreed to do what he could, and while still seeking legal authority of some kind to make the transfer, sounded Willkie out on the proposal. The emissary was William Allen White, the distinguished Republican editor from Kansas, who was also one of the leaders of the interventionist movement. Willkie agreed not to oppose the transfer, but neither did he agree to support it.

While the program was still in the rumor stage, Willkie made an announcement to the press that he would make no advance commitments on foreign policy if any were sought by the President.

In September Roosevelt notified Congress that he had agreed to trade fifty overage American destroyers to Britain for eight bases on British soil in the Western Hemisphere, mostly in the Caribbean where they would be helpful in defending the Panama Canal. The President armed himself with an opinion from Attorney General Robert Jackson holding that the President had the right to act without Congress passing a law to cover it.

Willkie's first public reaction was to declare that "the country undoubtedly will approve of the program. It is regrettable however that the President did not deem it necessary to seek the approval of Congress or permit public discussion prior to adoption." Willkie was correct in appraising the public reaction. Even the ultraisolationist *Chicago Tribune* hailed the deal as a "triumph," though adding that "it is sad to note that the motivating impulse was giving destroyers to England, not getting bases for ourselves." A major dissent came from the *St. Louis Post-Dispatch,* which editorially headlined, "Dictator Roosevelt Commits an Act of War."

Willkie's second reaction to the destroyer deal, only three days after his first, was less understandable. Apparently truckling to the isolationist sentiment without opposing the deal itself, he attacked Roosevelt's action as "the most dictatorial act ever taken by an American President," adding that "if I am President, I shall never lead the country into war."

The other war-connected item on which the nominees took positions was the passage of the Burke-Wadsworth Act, the nation's first peacetime conscription of men into the armed forces. This time they were in complete agreement, and yet Willkie again emerged with the lesser prestige.

Early in 1940 Roosevelt had let others, in and out of Congress, take the lead on the red-hot conscription issue, and it was not until early August that he came out for the first time, in a Washington press conference, for passage of the measure. Willkie, against the advice of many close to him, did the same in his Elwood speech two weeks later, while in between isolationist leaders like Senator Wheeler demanded a national referendum on conscription. Our professional Army at the moment numbered 270,000 men, short of the 375,000 authorized by Congress.

The Senate passed the bill, then calling for men between

the ages of twenty-one and thirty-one, before the end of August by the substantial majority of fifty-eight to thirty-one, but with an amendment permitting the government to seize industrial plants if they refused to cooperate in the defense effort. It was put into the bill as a sop to those who contended that if labor were being conscripted, so should capital. But Willkie chose to hit the new language as a step toward Sovietizing American industry, and a few days later as "a cheap political trick of the kind that brought France to its destruction." Roosevelt dismissed Willkie's position with the press conference remark that the Republicans were trying to drag the draft into politics.

Then the Republican isolationists in the House of Representatives kicked up a storm. Hamilton Fish, the ranking Republican member of the Military Affairs Committee, proposed to hold up the registration for draft until after Election Day, which would have had a two-month delay on the start toward a new Army. Willkie publicly opposed the Fish amendment.

But the final vote in Congress showed clearly that Willkie, in favoring the draft, did not speak with the same voice as the Republican leadership. In the Senate, 40 Democrats and 7 Republicans voted for the bill, while 13 Democrats and 10 Republicans opposed it. In the House, 186 Democrats and 46 Republicans voted yes, while 32 Democrats and 88 Republicans were in opposition.

The Republicans tried to come up with big names among the Democrats who opposed Roosevelt on the third-term issue, but without conspicuous success. They were able to rally Al Smith, John W. Davis and Bainbridge Colby—to list the most active and vocal—but these were men who had opposed Roosevelt's election for a second term. They had failed in 1936, and they attracted even less attention this time. John W. Hanes and Alan Valentine headed up a Democrats for Willkie organization, and George White, a former Democratic Governor of Ohio and former chairman of the Democratic National Committee, was an additional recruit. But they failed to get one man who might have helped more than all the rest—Jim Farley.

Farley, after having been over-ridden by the Roosevelt forces at the Democratic convention, immediately called for all to support the ticket. At the same time, he withdrew from all active participation in the campaign. He resisted all of Roosevelt's blandishments to recall his resignation as national chairman or as Postmaster General.

When Roosevelt came to New York in the final week of the campaign, protocol called for Farley to be at the meeting in his capacity as Democratic state chairman of New York. But Roosevelt went further and personally cajoled Farley into riding in his car through the city before the meeting, to be seen by all who saw the President. Also, Farley as state chairman had always sent out a personal telegram to all of the county chairmen on election eve, asking their best efforts for the ticket.

This routine message in 1940 was given national play in the newspapers, and had the effect of rallying the reluctant Farley to the Roosevelt cause. It probably helped in Irish communities, particularly in upstate New York. In Albany, the state capital, where Roosevelt had ruled as Governor, Willkie buttons were as common as dandelions on the Capitol lawn, yet by Election Day the O'Connell machine was able to round up its normal, heavy Democratic majority.

The trend of things abroad kept the public constantly alert to the theme of both parties that 1940 was a year of decision. Charles de Gaulle, coming into prominence as leader of the Fighting French—as opposed to those who had surrendered—was condemned to death, after a trial in absentia, by a Vichy French court just as the month of August began. Later that month saw the beginning of the daylight dogfights between the British RAF defenders, with their Hurricanes and Spitfires, and the German Messerschmidt invaders, battles that were described in detail every day in the American press. Only a matter of weeks later Hitler tried to burn out London by fires started from bombings, and the American public's heart went out to the underdog defenders.

In September Japan announced it had joined the Axis Powers

and would be a full ally of Germany and Italy in setting up a new world order. It did not enter the European war, but America's long-standing fear of the Japanese "Yellow Peril" was revived.

Total war raged in Europe throughout the fall as the Germans tried to break down British morale and defenses and the British in turn bombed Hamburg, Bremen and Berlin to bring war home to the Nazis. From the London Bureau of *The New York Times* the reports to America were identified, for office purposes, as "in raids" or "out raids."

The New York Times printed more political news in 1940 than any other newspaper. To give a flavor of the political infighting, I have summarized typical *Times* stories for the months of August, September, October and the first part of November, along with occasional war headlines which competed for first-page attention. In each case the date used is the date of publication:

Aug. 1 . . . Roosevelt signs bill for the expansion of the TVA at a cost of $68,000,000. Puts embargo on the export of aviation gasoline outside the Western Hemisphere.

. . . Virginio Gayda, Mussolini's spokesman in Rome, predicts a long war.

Aug. 2 . . . Bronx Boss Edward J. Flynn is elected chairman of the Democratic National Committee, succeeding Farley, who declines to manage a third-term campaign.

. . . Senators Rush D. Holt and Gerald P. Nye, Republicans, and Burton K. Wheeler, Democrat, address an anticonscription rally in Washington.

Aug. 3 . . . Roosevelt comes out for the first time for the Burke-Wadsworth selective service bill.

. . . Congress considers amortization provisions for defense plants. British counterraids leave Hamburg in ruins.

Aug. 4 . . . Gallup poll gives Roosevelt a slight popular edge, but sees 304 electoral votes, more than a majority, for Willkie.

. . . Henry P. Fletcher, counsel to Republican National

Committee, rules that Hatch Act limits on spending apply only to each committee, thus eliminating ceiling on spending and contributions. Willkie disagrees, and says money can be managed by using volunteers, rather than paid speakers.

Aug. 5 . . . Charles A. Lindbergh addresses forty thousand in Soldiers Field in Chicago, under auspices of the Citizens Committee to Keep America Out of War.

. . . General John J. Pershing, coming out of retirement, answers Lindbergh in radio address the same night.

Aug. 6 . . . Willkie, at Des Moines, urges decentralization of industry and defense plants.

. . . Congress' spending rises to twenty billion dollars.

. . . Army maneuvers, called "war games," start in Louisiana.

Aug. 8 . . . American newspaper reports from London show that the British and the Americans are already coordinating their war production efforts to ensure adequate supplies without duplication.

. . . Senator Harry S Truman holds a narrow lead over Governor Lloyd Stark in Missouri Democratic Senatorial primary.

Aug. 9 . . . Willkie announces that Tom Dewey will stump for the ticket.

. . . White House announces President will inspect naval bases at Portsmouth, Newport and New London.

. . . British shoot down fifty-six German planes over London.

Aug. 10 . . . Roosevelt, in discussing plans for federalizing the National Guard, says chances are one hundred to one against it being used in service abroad.

Aug. 11 . . . Senator Wheeler asks national referendum on conscription.

. . . Roosevelt tours Boston along routes well-advertised in advance. Tells cheering audience that the nation is really getting into stride on defense production.

. . . War Department figures show U.S. Army numbers 270,000, short of the 375,000 authorized by Congress.

Aug. 12 . . . German and British planes in dawn to dusk dogfights over the British channel as Hitler begins his aerial *blitzkrieg.*

Aug. 14 . . . Willkie, contrasting Republican and Democratic campaign chairmen, says he picked Joe Martin, "one of the outstanding public servants in America," while Roosevelt picked "Boss Flynn."

Aug. 15 . . . Joseph B. McWilliams, leader of the Christian Mobilizers, seeks Republican nomination for Congress from the German-Irish Yorkville section of New York.

Aug. 16 . . . Willkie, at Kansas City on his way to Elwood, assails corrupt political machines backing Roosevelt.

Aug. 17 . . . Roosevelt, at press conference, confirms discussions with England over Western Hemisphere bases, and plans for a joint defense organization with Canada. He leaves to inspect ninety thousand troops holding maneuvers at Ogdensburg, near the Canadian border.

Aug. 18 . . . Norman Thomas, veteran Socialist leader, describes Willkie's Elwood speech as a "synthesis of McGuffey's First Reader, the genealogy of Indiana, the collected speeches of Tom Girdler [antilabor steel executive] and *The New Republic.*"

Aug. 19 . . . The Ku Klux Klan holds an "Americanization meeting" at a headquarters of the German-American Bund in New Jersey.

. . . London reports Germans lost 140 of 600 planes raiding London that day.

. . . Roosevelt announces formation of U.S.-Canada Joint Board on Defense.

Aug. 20 . . . Gallup poll shows sixty-two to thirty-eight in favor of trading destroyers to Britain.

Aug. 21 . . . Roosevelt, in response to press conference question whether he will accept Willkie's challenge to debate, says that the White House reporters all know how busy he is with other things.

. . . Willkie retorts that no President has the right to eliminate discussion of the issues in a democracy.

Aug. 22 . . . Leon Trotsky is killed in Mexico City by an ice pick wielded by a Stalin agent.

Aug. 23 . . . Roosevelt and Canadian Prime Minister McKenzie King announce makeup of U.S.-Canada Joint Defense Board, with Mayor La Guardia of New York as a vice-chairman.

. . . Willkie announces details of eighteen-state campaign tour from Indiana to the Pacific Coast and back.

Aug. 24 . . . Roosevelt tells White House press conference that the pending draft bill should be enacted by Congress in the next two weeks. Sees armed forces needing 800,000 more men.

. . . Senate completes action on a bill to mobilize the National Guard for one year's training.

. . . Willkie lunches with Francis Cardinal Spellman at St. Patrick's Cathedral in New York.

. . . *Editor & Publisher* survey shows 66 per cent of the nation's press for Willkie, 20 per cent for Roosevelt and 14 per cent uncommitted.

Aug. 25 . . . Willkie urges creation here of a single Department of Defense, with divisions of the Army, and Navy and a new one for Air.

Aug. 26 . . . Gallup poll gives Willkie 284 electoral votes, coming from 20 states, and based on 49 per cent of the popular vote. Roosevelt trails in electoral votes with 247, but is credited with 28 states and 51 per cent of the popular vote.

Aug. 27 . . . The National Defense Advisory Commission reports orders placed for 6,747 planes for the Army and Navy, with rate of 10,000 a year growing to 36,000 a year by December, 1941.

. . . Willkie demands Roosevelt appoint a chairman of the

National Defense Advisory Commission, who would be the overall production boss.

Aug. 28 . . . *Social Justice*, organ of Father Charles E. Coughlin, endorses Willkie.

. . . Willkie declares he doesn't want Coughlin's support, or the "support of anybody who stands for any form of prejudice as to anybody's race or religion, or who is in support of any foreign economic or political philosophy in this country."

Aug. 29 . . . The Senate passes, by a vote of 58–31, the Burke-Wadsworth draft law, first peacetime conscription in the nation's history.

. . . Willkie hails renomination by California Republicans of Senator Hiram Johnson. Says Johnson, a leading isolationist, is one of America's "true Progressives."

Aug. 30 . . . Henry Wallace, accepting vice-presidential nomination, charges GOP is the party of appeasement.

. . . Willkie attacks the Overton-Russell amendment to the draft law, permitting plant seizure by the government, as a step toward "Sovietizing of American Industry."

. . . The British start bombing Berlin in retaliation for London raids.

Aug. 31 . . . Roosevelt tells press conference, when asked about Willkie's position on the Overton-Russell amendment, that the Republicans are trying to drag the draft into politics.

Sept. 1 . . . Flynn backs up Henry Wallace's charge that the GOP is the party of appeasement. Quotes German-American Bund papers as saying all good American Nazis should be for Willkie.

. . . Roosevelt issues Labor Day statement appealing for a common effort by business, labor and agriculture dedicated to the preservation of democracy.

Sept. 2 . . . Roosevelt issues call of sixty thousand National Guardsmen to active service as of September 16, the first time the Guard has been so directed.

Sept. 3 . . . Roosevelt, at the Great Smokies National Park, calls for national unity in the interests of "total defense." Press reports comment that his nonpolitical speeches and tour bear strong resemblance to his 1932 and 1936 campaign trips.

Sept. 4 . . . Roosevelt notifies Congress that he has traded fifty overage American destroyers for eight bases on British soil in the Western Hemisphere.

. . . Press dispatches from London report that "it is difficult to overstate the jubilation in England."

Sept. 5 . . . First official disclosure is made that America sent rifles, machine guns and cannon to England at the height of the invasion threat following Dunkirk.

Sept. 6 . . . Flynn says Willkie seeks the rule of the nation by Wall Street.

Sept. 7 . . . Willkie says destroyer-bases deal is "the most dictatorial act ever taken by an American President."

Sept. 9 . . . Germans stage worst raid yet on London, leaving the city in blaze all night.

Sept. 10 . . . Roosevelt, signing $5 billion arms bill, biggest in history, says it insures 200 more ships for a two-ocean navy, including 7 battleships and 8 airplane carriers.

Sept. 11 . . . British planes bomb the Reichstag building in Berlin while the Nazis hit London for eight successive hours.

. . . Republican hopes buoyed by results of Maine gubernatorial election, in which they got 64.5 per cent of the vote, highest since 1928.

Sept. 12 . . . Roosevelt makes his first "political speech" to the Teamsters Union, reviewing what the New Deal has done for the past eight years in improving the life of the laboring man.

. . . Press reports from Rome say that the Italian radio and newspapers are hailing the "Willkie victory" in Maine, on the theory that Roosevelt is a known evil, while Willkie is at least a doubtful one.

Sept. 14 . . . German bombs hit Buckingham Palace, residence of the King and Queen.

. . . Willkie tours Chicago and its suburbs.

Sept. 15 . . . Congress gives final approval to Burke-Wadsworth draft law.

. . . Willkie shows hoarseness in Joliet speech attacking Roosevelt for supporting Munich pact; throat specialist is rushed to campaign train.

Sept. 16 . . . British fighters down 185 German planes, many of them landing in the streets of London.

. . . Willkie's aides are reported uneasy about effectiveness of their candidate's early campaigning tactics.

Sept. 17 . . . Roosevelt signs the draft law, setting October 16 as registration day for 16,000,000 men aged 21 through 35. Sees 400,000 to be called for training before January 1.

. . . Willkie at Coffeyville says FDR has lost faith in the American people and that if he is re-elected, America will be under a totalitarian government before the end of the third term.

. . . Secretary of State Cordell Hull answers Willkie on Munich, saying that charge was "untrue and makes it evident that he is grossly ignorant of the history of the last few years."

Sept. 18 . . . Willkie, at Amarillo, Texas, says South must choose between its traditions based on Democracy and the third-term candidacy.

. . . Gallup poll says Willkie has slipped in New York, New Jersey and Pennsylvania to the extent that Roosevelt now leads in those states.

Sept. 19 . . . Herbert Hoover in speech at the University of Pennsylvania says America's entry into World War II would result in total dictatorship here.

. . . The Steuben Society, leading German-American group, backs Willkie as opposed to dictatorships.

. . . *The New York Times* makes the first endorsement of a Republican presidential nominee in its history, basing it on Willkie as the man better equipped to defend America while employing sound fiscal policies, and also because of the paper's opposition to breaking the no-third-term tradition.

Sept. 20 . . . Willkie in Los Angeles says he proposes to rescue America from an incompetent administration.

. . . Gallup poll shows Roosevelt carrying 38 states to Willkie's 10, for electoral college totals of 453 to 78.

Sept. 21 . . . Roosevelt, in a "nonpolitical" address at the University of Pennsylvania, answers the dictatorship charge with the statement that a free election is the greatest safeguard for democracy, adding: "No dictator in history has ever dared run the gauntlet of a really free election." He tours the Philadelphia Navy Yard and notes that it is employing nineteen thousand men, against eight thousand a year before.

Sept. 22 . . . The Census Bureau puts the population of the United States at 131,409,881.

Sept. 23 . . . Willkie tells press he is happy over the first half of his Western swing, although press notes that heckling and booing has been increasing.

Sept. 24 . . . British and Free French attack Dakar, in attempt to wrest French fleet there from Vichy control.

. . . Roosevelt sends letters to forty-eight state governors, asking them to set up local draft machinery.

Sept. 25 . . . Senator Norris and Mayor La Guardia stage, at the White House, the organization of the Independent Committee for Roosevelt.

. . . Willkie, in Butte, Montana, lashes out at centralization of government.

Sept. 26 . . . Harold Ickes hits Willkie as a candidate who is a friend of public power in the West and a foe of public power in Wall Street.

Sept. 27 . . . Roosevelt orders an embargo on the export of scrap iron except to Great Britain and countries in the Western Hemisphere. Principal target of the order is Japan.

. . . The Dewey machine in New York yields to a personal plea by Willkie and schedules Representative Bruce Barton as its nominee for U.S. Senator.

Sept. 29 . . . Willkie, at Republican state convention in New York nominating Barton, says that the time has come for government to cease giving to the people, and for people to start giving to the government.

Sept. 30 . . . Willkie leaves New York for five-day swing through Indiana, Ohio, Michigan and Pennsylvania.

. . . Dewey, Taft, Bricker, Hoover, Landon, Stassen and Theodore Roosevelt, Jr., all schedule speaking tours for the Republican ticket.

Oct. 1 . . . Governor Lehman of New York, addressing the Democratic state convention there, says that nothing that could happen in the United States could give Hitler, Mussolini and Stalin and the government of Japan more satisfaction than the defeat of Roosevelt.

. . . Willkie gets chilly reception on Michigan tour, including barrage of missiles thrown at his caravan.

Oct. 2 . . . Willkie says Lehman statement is "innuendo that is false, malicious and subversive, tending to destroy national unity."

. . . Flynn deplores stone-throwing at Willkie train, saying he is "distressed and disgusted."

Oct. 3 . . . Willkie in Cleveland charges Roosevelt with playing politics with national defense.

. . . Lehman says his speech was a clear statement of fact, and did not impugn Willkie's patriotism.

Oct. 4 . . . Willkie makes his labor speech in Pittsburgh, giving a seven-point program for local controls and decentralization of bureaucracy.

Oct. 5 . . . Willkie in Philadelphia says Roosevelt's declaration that 1,700 tanks were "on hand or on order" counted 1,500 tanks not in existence.

. . . Roosevelt, at press conference, calls attention to a *New York Times* story from Rome saying that the Axis Powers would like to see him defeated.

Oct. 6 . . . Willkie, at meetings in Brooklyn, denounces the "whispering campaign" being waged against him.

. . . The Gallup poll reports Roosevelt ahead in forty-two states, and Willkie ahead in six, with Roosevelt getting 56 per cent of the popular vote. However, poll says Roosevelt is losing momentum.

Oct. 7 . . . Roosevelt tours defense installations in the Albany-Schenectady area of New York State, with his caravan going through jammed streets and cheering crowds.

Oct. 9 . . . Willkie, in The Bronx, hits Roosevelt's credibility, and demands to know if there are any secret understandings committing the nation to war.

Oct. 10 . . . Willkie gets a warm reception on auto tour of Connecticut.

Oct. 11 . . . The Nazis begin to take over the Balkans.

. . . Total air war rages over London.

. . . Roosevelt leaves Washington for a tour of defense plants and preparations in Pennsylvania and Ohio.

Oct. 13 . . . Roosevelt, in Dayton, makes a major foreign policy speech, declaring America not only will defend the Western Hemisphere, but "we include the right to the peaceful use of the Atlantic and Pacific Oceans."

Oct. 14 . . . Flynn disclaims a circular issued by Democratic Negro division, which attacked Willkie's German ancestry and accused his father of responsibility for Jim Crow rules in Elwood.

Oct. 15 . . . The Gallup poll reports a shift of Illinois, Indiana and Michigan to Willkie and adds that "the campaign has many of the elements of a horse race, as it enters the final stretch."

. . . Colonel Lindbergh appeals for "the election of leaders we can trust, who will lead us to strength and peace, rather than weakness and war."

Oct. 16 . . . Willkie, on eve of draft registration, says nation has an obligation to those going into training to see that they are provided "with the finest equipment and when their service is over, have opportunity for a good job, to earn a living, marry and get ahead."

Oct. 17 . . . Roosevelt presides over nation's first peacetime conscription, which he likens to a mustering of Colonial militia.

Oct. 18 . . . Willkie, in St. Louis, says Administration is so far behind in defense production that it cannot supply either British or our own needs.

Oct. 19 . . . Roosevelt schedules his first five "political speeches" between October 23 and November 2 to answer opposition, saying they are engaged in "systematic and deliberate falsification of the facts."

Oct. 20 . . . Gallup poll says Roosevelt had 51 per cent and Willkie 49 per cent of popular vote on August 4, but that percentages now are Roosevelt 55, Willkie 45.

Oct. 23 . . . Willkie, in Chicago, hammers away at danger of Roosevelt leading the nation into war.

. . . Gallup poll says Willkie would be leading Roosevelt by 6 per cent in the popular vote if it weren't for the war.

Oct. 24 . . . Al Smith, at meeting in Brooklyn, assails Roosevelt as "the chief apostle of class hatred in the United States."

. . . Roosevelt, in first political speech in Philadelphia, laces into opposition for using "the technique of the big lie."

Oct. 26 . . . John L. Lewis delivers bitter attack on Roosevelt as a "traitor to labor."

. . . Henry A. Wallace characterizes Willkie as "well-meaning, confused, and supported by Nazi agents."

Oct. 27 . . . Lewis speech repudiated by overwhelming majority of CIO leaders.

Oct. 29 . . . Roosevelt, in Madison Square Garden speech, answers critics of defense production. Develops major slogan for Democrats in citing "Martin, Barton and Fish" for isolationist votes in Congress.

Oct. 30 . . . Joseph P. Kennedy, American Ambassador to

Britain, makes radio speech declaring Roosevelt has made no secret commitments to bring the nation into the war and says rearming is the best way to keep us out.

Oct. 31 . . . Roosevelt, in Boston speech, repeats attack on Martin, Barton and Fish, and reminds audience that "again and again and again" he has pledged American troops would not be sent to fight "in any foreign wars."

Nov. 1 . . . Henry Wallace, at Madison Square Garden rally of New York's American Labor Party, says Hitler wants Willkie to defeat Roosevelt.

. . . Herbert Hoover, in Lincoln, Nebraska, says Roosevelt's "billingsgate" in addressing heads of other nations has cost the U.S. its moral influence in the world.

Nov. 2 . . . Roosevelt, in Brooklyn Academy of Music address, sees extreme radicals and extreme reactionaries in an "unholy alliance" to elect Willkie.

. . . Secretary of State Hull makes radio speech saying the country needs Roosevelt.

Nov. 3 . . . *The New York Times* forecast of the election result gives Roosevelt 231 electoral votes, Willkie 111, and leaves 189 in doubt, with 266 required for an electoral majority. The forecast told of reports from *Times* correspondents that showed a Republican trend in enough doubtful areas to make Willkie's election possible.

. . . Willkie, in final New York speech, sees "The Battle of America" having been won in the campaign just ending.

. . . Roosevelt, in final major speech at Cleveland, paints a picture of his own faith in the future of democracy and predicts great gains for the common good in the years ahead by continuation of New Deal reforms.

Nov. 4 . . . Democratic Chairman Ed Flynn predicts 427 electoral votes, and all but nine states for Roosevelt; Republican Chairman Joe Martin predicts 324 for Willkie, but does not name states.

. . . The Gallup poll gives Roosevelt 52 per cent of vote, to 48 per cent for Willkie, but says because of lopsided Southern totals, a Democratic candidate needs more than 52 per cent to be sure of winning. Sees possibility that candidate with popular majority might still lose, especially in view of "strong trend" for Willkie that was still running. The Gallup poll gave Roosevelt 198 sure electoral votes, and Willkie 59, with 19 states and 274 electoral votes in doubt.

. . . The *Fortune* poll, run by Elmo Roper, gave Roosevelt 55.2 per cent of the popular vote, but said Willkie was gaining.

. . . Willkie, in a statement from his New York apartment, pledges enactment of a constitutional amendment barring any President from ever again seeking a third term.

. . . Roosevelt rests and relaxes at Hyde Park estate.

Nov. 5 . . . Willkie, in final radio broadcast, says that the re-election of Roosevelt would mean that "the last step in the destruction of our democracy has been taken."

. . . Roosevelt tells his Dutchess County neighbors that "it is the last time, very obviously, that I will visit you as a candidate."

11 Totaling Up

State	Electoral Vote Roosevelt	Electoral Vote Willkie	Popular Vote Roosevelt	Popular Vote Willkie	Majority
Alabama	11		250,726	42,174	208,552
Arizona	3		95,267	54,030	41,237
Arkansas	9		158,622	42,121	116,501
California	22		1,877,618	1,351,417	526,211
Colorado		6	265,554	279,576	14,022
Connecticut	8		417,621	361,021	56,600
Delaware	3		74,599	61,440	13,159
Florida	7		359,334	126,158	233,176
Georgia	12		265,194	23,934	241,260
Idaho	4		127,842	106,553	21,289
Illinois	29		2,149,934	2,047,240	102,690
Indiana		14	874,073	899,466	25,393
Iowa		11	578,800	632,370	63,570
Kansas		9	364,725	489,169	124,444
Kentucky	11		557,222	410,384	146,838
Louisiana	10		319,751	52,446	267,305

State	Electoral Vote Roosevelt	Electoral Vote Willkie	Popular Vote Roosevelt	Popular Vote Willkie	Majority
Maine		5	156,478	165,951	9,473
Maryland	8		384,546	289,534	95,012
Massachusetts	17		1,076,552	939,700	136,852
Michigan		19	1,032,991	1,039,917	6,926
Minnesota	11		644,195	596,274	47,921
Mississippi	9		168,252	7,364	160,888
Missouri	15		958,476	871,009	87,477
Montana	4		145,698	99,579	46,119
Nebraska		7	263,677	352,201	88,524
Nevada	3		31,945	21,229	10,614
New Hampshire	4		125,292	110,127	15,165
New Jersey	16		1,016,404	944,876	71,528
New Mexico	3		103,699	79,315	24,384
New York	47		3,251,918	3,027,478	224,540
North Carolina	13		609,015	213,663	395,352
North Dakota		4	124,036	154,590	30,554
Ohio	26		1,733,139	1,586,773	146,366
Oklahoma	11		474,313	348,872	125,441
Oregon	5		258,415	219,655	39,760
Pennsylvania	36		2,171,035	1,889,848	281,187
Rhode Island	4		182,182	132,653	49,529
South Carolina	8		95,470	1,727	93,743
South Dakota		4	131,862	177,065	45,203
Tennessee	11		351,601	169,153	182,448
Texas	23		840,151	199,152	640,999
Utah	4		154,277	93,151	61,126
Vermont		3	64,269	78,371	14,102
Virginia	11		235,961	109,363	126,598
Washington	8		462,145	322,123	140,022
West Virginia	8		495,662	372,414	123,248
Wisconsin	12		704,281	679,260	25,021
Wyoming	3		59,287	52,633	6,654
Totals	449	82	27,243,466	22,304,755	
				Roosevelt net margin	4,938,711

The official figures for the 1940 election gave Roosevelt 27,243,466—55 per cent of the popular vote—with which he carried 38 of the 48 states and amassed 449 votes in the Electoral College. Willkie drew 22,304,755—45 per cent—and was credited with 82 electoral votes from 10 states. Roosevelt's popular majority was 4,938,711.

Those were the figures of the official canvass, completed thirty days after election. But the unofficial and still incomplete returns on Wednesday morning, November 6, indicated that the two candidates were closer in the popular vote and farther apart in the electoral totals, so much so that the lead news story in *The New York Times,* written and signed by its Washington Bureau chief, Arthur Krock, read:

> Over an apparently huge popular minority, which under the electoral college system was not able to register its proportion of the total vote in terms of electors, President Roosevelt was chosen yesterday for a third term, the first American in history to break the tradition which began with the Republic. . . .

At that moment, the figures available showed that Roosevelt had sewed up 429 electoral votes, Willkie 53, and 49 were placed in the doubtful column. For the next several days, close states, particularly Michigan and Indiana, shifted to Willkie, to Roosevelt and back again as the count continued, and the voting public turned its attention to newer developments, on the war or home fronts, before the final statistics emerged. The effect of this was to give the actual result a somewhat blurred image, in which Willkie admirers such as Krock saw nothing but their candidate's record Republican popular vote, while members of the Dewey and Taft "I told you so" claques dwelt on Willkie's relatively slender electoral college total.

In cold analysis, Willkie supporters had no unique reason to complain of the translation of popular votes into electoral votes. A tabulation of the results in Roosevelt's four presidential campaigns shows up as follows:

Year	Opponent	Popular Vote %	Electoral Votes	Electoral %
1932	Hoover	40.5	59	11
1936	Landon	37.5	8	1.5
1940	Willkie	45	82	15
1944	Dewey	46	99	18.6

Willkie's only chance of winning, recognized by his own backers from the very start, lay in the quirks of the electoral college system which permit the election of one candidate even though his opponent received more popular support, as witness the election of Benjamin Harrison over Grover Cleveland in 1888. This was an advantage open only to the Republicans, since it could eventuate only from the waste of popular votes of the Democrats in running up top-heavy majorities in the Southern states.

The Gallup poll, in hedging its prediction of the 1940 result, had leaned heavily on what it called the axiom that the Democratic nominee for President, any year, needed a minimum of 52 per cent of the popular vote even to be in the running. The pollster, as well as Willkie's backers, saw that Willkie's hope lay in majorities, narrow or otherwise, in a dozen of the industrial and industrial-farm states lying north of the Ohio and east of the Mississippi. These were the battleground states, each of which he was conceded a chance of winning. He did carry two of them. Had he carried them all—completed a twelve-horse parlay and held his winnings elsewhere—he would have been President.

It is even possible to show that he came close. A transfer of 600,000 Roosevelt votes to Willkie, carefully spotted in the 10 states, would have done it. Willkie would have wound up with 281 electoral votes, a majority of 15, while Roosevelt retained a popular majority of 3,700,000.

That kind of juggling can, of course, be made to work in reverse. If fewer than 225,000 votes were taken from Willkie and transferred to Roosevelt in the 10 other states that Willkie did carry, Willkie would still have had the greatest popular vote cast up to then for a Republican nominee—exceeded first by Eisenhower in 1952—and would have wound up with an absolute zero in the Electoral College.

To explain the 1940 vote and result, it helps to take the nation apart into voting units or targets. First, a look at what used to be—and in 1940, still was—the "Solid South." It consisted of the 11 states which seceded from the Union in early 1861, following Lincoln's election as President. They were Alabama, Arkansas, Florida, Georgia, Louisiana, Mississippi, North Carolina, South Carolina, Tennessee, Texas and Virginia. Republican enclaves existed in the mountains of western North Carolina and eastern Tennessee, but the voting habits of the rest are best described by the apochryphal story of the political pollster who asked an aged Southerner how he usually voted. The answer was:

"I vote the way I shot."

The Solid South became a national political unit after the Union troops were pulled out of the would-be secessionist states following the election of 1876, and the white residents became free to run their own elections. The one-time Confederacy became a one-party area in which all contests for local or state office were settled in the Democratic primary, and the vote for the Democratic nominee for President was automatic. There were only two presidential elections from 1880 to 1940 which presented exceptions.

In 1920, the Harding landslide, bringing the nation "back to normalcy," had enough pull to draw Tennessee out of the Democratic and into the Republican column. In 1928 it was the religious issue. The Protestant South was asked for the first time to support a Catholic for President on the Democratic ticket. In four states—Florida, North Carolina, Tennessee and Texas—there were enough Southern bigots who believed Ku Klux Klan propaganda that Al Smith, if elected, would move the Pope of Rome into the White House, to shift those states—for that election only—into the Republican electoral column.

The 1940 campaign presented no such religious issue. The

battle between Northern and Southern Democrats over civil rights for the Negro did not become an election issue until 1948. The South in 1940 still had an economy based on cotton exports to Europe and was internationalist—and Roosevelt did exceptionally well in the returns.

State	Roosevelt	Willkie	Majority for Roosevelt
Alabama	250,726	42,174	208,552
Arkansas	158,622	42,121	116,501
Florida	359,334	126,158	233,176
Georgia	265,194	23,934	241,260
Louisiana	319,751	52,241	267,510
Mississippi	168,252	7,364	160,888
North Carolina	609,015	213,663	395,352
South Carolina	95,470	1,727	93,743
Tennessee	351,601	169,153	182,448
Texas	840,151	199,152	640,999
Virginia	235,961	109,363	126,598
Totals	3,654,077	987,050	2,667,027

The Southern majority for Roosevelt amounted to 54 per cent of his nationwide popular margin, and gave him every one of the area's 124 electoral votes. Willkie had originally planned to stump the South. His final judgment was not to waste his time there, and he made only one speech, at Amarillo, in the more-West-than-South Texas Panhandle.

A far more promising—and productive—target was the "farm belt," the corn and wheat producing states of Iowa, Kansas, Minnesota, Nebraska, North Dakota and South Dakota. Southern Indiana, southern Illinois, Wisconsin and Missouri, while similar, were in a different political category because of their great cities that could neutralize the rural influence. In 1940 the nation's farm population was still tremendous, and the so-called farm vote had historically been of concern to every nominee of every party.

This was true even though the farm states were almost as notoriously and consistently Republican as the Southern states were Democratic. They could be wooed away from their Republicanism if their complaints about their economic rewards were particularly justified. But the farmer, when really dissatisfied, was more likely to vote Populist or Progressive than Democratic. The first time he switched en masse to the Democrats was in 1932, when he had dropped from poor to poverty-stricken on the economic totem pole. He voted Democratic again in 1936, in return for the Roosevelt farm-subsidy program under the AAA, which showed that government could do something for the farmer if it were so disposed.

But the record over the years had shown that the farmer did revert to Republicanism when the point of his grievance had been blunted, and Willkie's 1940 showing was not surprising. Willkie campaigned extensively in every one of the six highly rural farm states, with this result:

State	Roosevelt	Willkie	Margin
Iowa	578,800	632,370	63,570
Kansas	364,725	489,169	124,444
Minnesota	644,195	596,274	47,921 (R)
Nebraska	263,677	352,201	88,524
North Dakota	124,036	154,590	30,554
South Dakota	131,662	177,065	45,203
	2,107,095	2,401,669	

Willkie's votes in the farm belt gave him his only sectional popular majority, 294,574, five of the six states, and 35 of its 46 electoral votes. It may be noted, in passing, that the whole area cast fewer popular votes and was entitled to fewer electoral votes than the single state of New York.

Minnesota ran against the farm state trend and into the Roosevelt column because of its great Scandinavian population. Normally Republican, the Norwegians and Danes, as well as most of the Swedes, were personally and emotionally involved in the battle against Hitler, and thus were highly interventionist.

Looking westward from the farm belt in 1940 were the Rocky Mountain group of Arizona, Colorado, Idaho, Montana, Nevada, New Mexico, Utah and Wyoming, eight states whose slender congressional representation entitled them to a mere twenty-seven electoral college votes. They had in common a tendency to shift from Democratic to Republican and back again, usually winding up with the national winner. Four of the eight, Idaho, Montana, Nevada and Wyoming, had cast more votes for Robert La Follette, Progressive, than for John W. Davis, Democrat, in the 1924 Coolidge election, indicating an aversion to Wall Street nominees. No one paid them much mind in the 1940 campaign, and all but Colorado wound up in the Roosevelt column, with Colorado showing more consistent Republican voting in the elections that followed.

On the Pacific Coast, California in 1940 had only twenty-two electoral votes, less than half of what it was to rate in 1968. Oregon with five and Washington with eight electoral votes brought the total up to thirty-five. While Willkie campaigned in all three Pacific Coast states on his first Western tour, he never had a chance of making a dent. California was in the process of building up the giant Democratic registration majority that made the Republicans depend on Democratic feuds for election day successes; Oregon and Washington had strong liberal, even radical traditions which drew them naturally closer to the New Deal than Willkie's Republicanism. In addition, great airplane and ship-building industries were coming into being, resolving the unemployment problems and creating a more widespread prosperity than ever before.

The Pacific Coast vote was:

State	Roosevelt	Willkie	Margin
California	1,877,618	1,351,417	526,201
Oregon	258,415	219,665	38,750
Washington	462,145	322,123	140,022
	2,598,178	1,893,205	704,973

Roosevelt's majority in California was second only to his margin in Texas, and those two states together gave him more of a victory, in terms of popular margins, than the ten battleground states which decided the election.

The next identifiable bloc consists of the "border" states of Delaware, Maryland, West Virginia, Kentucky, Missouri and Oklahoma, torn at election time between Northern and Southern influences, and with a total of fifty-six electoral votes. West Virginia and Kentucky had enough coal miners and other underprivileged to be counted from the start in the Roosevelt column. In Missouri, the only question was whether the dying Pendergast machine in Kansas City could out-vote—once its padded election rolls had been purged—the Republican tendencies of the St. Louis Germans and the farmers in the rural areas. Oklahoma had left the Democratic ticket only in 1920, for normalcy, and in 1928, against Smith, Delaware had cast its little vote for the popular vote winner in every election except 1932, when the influence of the DuPont empire kept it in the Hoover column.

In 1940, no one expected them to leave the Democratic Party, and they didn't.

State	Roosevelt	Willkie	Margin
Delaware	74,599	61,440	13,159
Kentucky	557,222	410,334	146,888
Maryland	384,546	289,534	95,012
Missouri	958,476	878,009	80,467
Oklahoma	474,313	348,872	125,441
West Virginia	495,662	372,414	123,248
	2,944,818	2,360,603	584,215

Roosevelt's 584,215 margin, properly spread out, gave him every one of the border states.

The region that settled the 1940 election—and which could have settled it differently without a revolutionary change in past voting habits—was north of the Ohio River and east of the Mississippi River, containing most of the big states in the Union. It included 14 states—Maine, New Hampshire, Vermont, Massachussetts, Rhode Island, Connecticut, New York, New Jersey, Pennsylvania, Ohio, Indiana, Illinois, Wisconsin and Michigan—entitled, on the basis of the congressional apportionment as it existed in 1940, to 240 of the 531 electoral college votes, just 26 votes short of an absolute majority.

They consistently supplied the Republicans with the popular and electoral college majorities which kept the GOP on top in the nation until the arrival of Franklin D. Roosevelt and the New Deal. Several of them had not gone Democratic since the Civil War, until the Roosevelt revolution of the 1930's. It is worth looking back at their voting records at least as far as 1912:

Maine—Went Democratic for Woodrow Wilson in 1912 only because of the division of the normally Republican vote between William Howard Taft and Teddy Roosevelt; otherwise was Republican in every election from 1860 to the Goldwater debacle of 1964.

New Hampshire—Democratic in 1912 on the basis of the GOP split; stayed with Wilson by the margin of 65 votes in 1916, and went Democratic for Roosevelt in 1936, 1940, 1944 and for Lyndon Johnson in 1964.

Vermont—Even more rockribbed Republican than Maine, Vermont voted for Taft in 1912, with Wilson running third. It never went Democratic until 1964.

Massachusetts—Democratic for Wilson in 1912 because of the GOP split, it went Democratic again in 1928 when its heavy Catholic vote swung the state to Al Smith, against the regional trend. It stayed in the Democratic column thereafter except for the Eisenhower years, 1952 and 1956.

Rhode Island—Followed the Massachusetts pattern exactly, and for the same reasons.

Connecticut—Went Democratic in 1912, only because of the GOP split; went Democratic for Roosevelt in 1936, 1940 and 1944, for John F. Kennedy in 1960 and Johnson in 1964.

New York—Went Democratic in 1912, only because of the GOP split; returned to the Democratic column for all four Roosevelt elections. In 1948 it went Republican for Dewey, for Eisenhower the next two elections, and Democratic in 1960 and 1964.

New Jersey—Duplicated the New York record.

Pennsylvania—Never went Democratic, from 1860 up to 1936. Even in 1912, Teddy Roosevelt carried the state, with Wilson second and Taft third. It stayed with Hoover in 1932—by just about the margin of votes the old GOP state machine could steal—and thereafter followed the New York-New Jersey pattern, Democratic in 1936, 1940, 1944, 1960 and 1964.

Ohio—Democratic for Wilson in 1912 and again in 1916. Reverted to the Democrats for Roosevelt's first three elections in 1932, 1936 and 1940; went for Truman in 1948 and Johnson in 1964.

Indiana—Like the rest, and for the same reasons, Democratic in 1912, and again in 1932 and 1936, but not again until 1964.

Illinois—Democratic in 1912, returned to the Democratic column in 1932 and stayed there through 1964, except for the Eisenhower years.

Wisconsin—Went Democratic in 1912 and was carried by Robert M. La Follette's Progressive ticket in 1924, with Republican Calvin Coolidge second, and John W. Davis, Democrat, a distant third. Thereafter went Democratic in 1932, 1936, 1940, 1948 and 1964.

Michigan—Was so traditionally non-Democratic that it even voted for Teddy Roosevelt in 1912, with Taft second and Wilson third. Went Democratic thereafter in 1932, 1936, 1944, 1960 and 1964.

Thus it can be seen that, up to the time the votes were counted in the Willkie-Roosevelt race, the Democratic voting records in the area were of recent vintage. They dated back, except for Massachusetts and Rhode Island, no more than the two previous presidential elections.

All of the states except Maine, Vermont and New Hampshire had substantial urban populations with voting tendencies normally opposite to those in rural territory, yet in the 1940 election there were crosscurrents of racial voting which affected both the city streets and the country acres. This prevented a clear-cut division of the vote along economic lines. There were many isolationists in the working class—Democratic since 1932—and many interventionists among the rich who had opposed so many of the economic practices of the Roosevelt New Deal.

Even though there was so little difference in the party platforms, and though Roosevelt's and Willkie's statements were equally firm in pledging to keep the nation out of war, the Democratic ticket was identified by the voters as more interventionist and the Republican ticket as more isolationist.

This identification, which resulted in much crossing of party lines, was accepted because of the isolationist charges the Democrats had heaped on the Republicans and the interventionist—warmonger—charges the Republicans had piled back on the Democrats, rather than anything the parties or the candidates said in their own behalf.

In some parts of the area, the interventionist label was worth votes to the Democrats because of the racial background of the population; in others it was costly, for the same reasons.

Interventionism reacted unexpectedly in behalf of the Democrats even in Maine and Vermont, not really regarded as part of the battleground because they were such traditionally Republican enclaves. No one gave the Democrats a chance to win them in 1940, yet they lost by much smaller margins than anyone anticipated.

Take Vermont. It had given Alf Landon as big a majority in the losing year of 1936 as it did Herbert Hoover in the Republican sweep of 1928. In the 1940 race, it gave Willkie three thousand votes fewer than Landon, and upped Roosevelt's vote by nearly forty thousand. Willkie thus squeaked through by fourteen thousand. Vermonters had British and Scotch bloodlines dating back to Colonial days, and French-speaking Canadians from Quebec. Among both groups, the fate of England and of France was of sufficient concern to swing many of them into the Democratic voting column for the first time in their lives.

Much the same was true in Maine. That state, in those years, held its gubernatorial election in September and its results were supposed to indicate the presidential vote that would follow in November. In 1940, Maine cast its heaviest Republican vote for governor since 1928—bucking up the morale of the GOP all around the nation. But when the November vote was counted, Willkie's nine thousand majority was the slenderest for a Republican nominee since that of Hughes in 1916. The contrast between the gubernatorial and presidential votes indicated that many Maine Republicans voted for the more interventionist candidate for President for the same reasons and in the same proportions as Vermont.

New Hampshire, which had slid into the Roosevelt column in 1936 for the first time since the Woodrow Wilson era, gave Roosevelt in 1940 a larger majority than its neighbor, Vermont, was able to muster for Willkie. The same racial factors which existed in Vermont worked in New Hampshire, plus the effect of the increase in employment and production in the paper and fabric mills.

Massachusetts and Rhode Island presented some different factors. The Republican hopes of carrying either or both lay in the hostility of the Irish-American to the English, and there were plenty of normally Democratic Irish in Boston and Providence. But whatever defections there were from the Democratic ranks of the urban Irish caused by Roosevelt's support of England, were counterbalanced by Republican interventionist voters in western Massachusetts and among the French-Canadians of Rhode Island's mill towns. Connecticut, last of the New England states, had a booming defense industry, with submarine installations at New London and airplane motor plants up and down the Connecticut River Valley. They served to overcome the state's long-time attachment to conservative Republicanism, and even the vote of the commuter from Fairfield County to Manhattan's Wall Street.

The vote pattern in New York, the biggest electoral prize of all with its 47 votes, was at least as complicated as any other in the union. Roosevelt polled a majority totaling 718,459 in three boroughs of New York City—Manhattan, Brooklyn and the Bronx—while suffering a net loss in each of the other two. The three suburban counties of Westchester, Nassau and Suffolk gave Willkie a total majority of 175,000, which was very respectable, but less than had been expected from these wealthy, commuter-run areas. But in the suburbs and the rest of upstate New York, Willkie's total margin as only 494,019 instead of a hoped-for 700,000, with the result that he lost the state by 224,440 in a total vote of nearly 6,300,000.

The discernible factors were the following:

Irish-Catholic Democrats, who had started defecting from the Democratic Party on local and state issues as early as 1936, departed in great numbers in 1940, with the isolation issue bringing it into full flower in New York City itself. But the Irish defection was offset by virtually unanimous support from the city's immense Jewish population. This showed up particularly in Brooklyn (Kings County) which with its 1,100,000 voters was the biggest Democratic voting unit in the United States. Roosevelt carried it by a whopping 350,000, but the three of Brooklyn's 23 wards which were predominantly Irish-Catholic each went Republican within its boundaries, even electing Republican legislators besides voting for Willkie, for the first time in their history.

Upstate, the iron hand of the O'Connell machine kept Albany's Irish in line for Roosevelt, even though Willkie buttons had been numerous. Rural Clinton County, on the Canadian border, went Democratic as a result of its French-Canadian population. In Erie County, Buffalo's Poles swung in behind Roosevelt, and defense-plant workers and garment industry labor in the chain of upstate cities along the line of the old Erie Canal helped neutralize the Republican vote from the villages, towns and farms.

New Jersey gave Roosevelt a respectable majority considering that a close watch was kept on Frank Hague's Jersey City machine—noted for ballot-box stuffing—and the noted Boss was able to produce only 102,000 majority for Roosevelt there, instead of the 170,000 he had predicted. The commuter vote for Willkie, obvious in the results from half the commuter territory, was balanced by union labor in the other half.

Pennsylvania, for so many years the keystone of Eastern Republicanism, gave Roosevelt the largest majority of any of the battleground states for a number of reasons. New and alert Democratic machines had replaced the old Republican ones in running Philadelphia and Pittsburgh, with the result that Roosevelt carried Philadelphia by 175,000—instead of losing it—and Allegheny County, which includes Pittsburgh, by more than 100,000.

The steps the Roosevelt Administration had taken to raise the standard of living of the coal miners put the coal counties in the Roosevelt column, even though it meant the miners were repudiating John L. Lewis.

Ohio, Indiana and Illinois were the states where isolationist sentiment was counted on by the Republicans to deliver the state to them. Many of the leading political figures, such as Taft in Ohio, were spokesmen for the theory that the war in Europe was none of our business, no matter who won it. Indiana had been run for years by a tight Republican state machine in which the Ku Klux Klan figured importantly, and the McNutt Democratic regime in the state capitol was regarded by most Hoosiers as a passing thing. Illinois was the home base for the America First Committee, the nation's leading isolationist organization, and also of Colonel Robert R. McCormick's *Chicago Tribune,* the leading organ of isolationism among the nation's press. Its influence spread from Chicago into Indiana and up to Wisconsin.

In evaluating campaigning as a factor in stimulating voter interest, it is worth noting that Roosevelt—who made a major speech in Cleveland at the very end of his campaign—did proportionately far better in Ohio than he did in Illinois and Indiana, which he never entered. On the other hand, Willkie campaigned up and down all three states, and carried only Indiana by a nose. Home state pride, notorious among Hoosiers, probably played a part.

The isolationist vote was discernible in Illinois, particularly in Cook County, which includes Chicago. The Kelly-Nash machine, plus the CIO unions, were able to muster only a 300,000 majority to offset Republican downstate by only a little over 100,000, one of the closest margins in decades for that state.

In Wisconsin, isolationism was of long standing. Even at the time of World War I, its congressional delegation stood out among the handful who voted against Wilson's declaration of war on the Kaiser's Germany. On the other hand, it had been one of the most progressive states of the Union in viewing the domestic economy, anticipating many New Deal reforms in its own state legislation. It had welcomed Roosevelt's 1932 and 1936 candidacies with thundering majorities, even though the Democratic Party in Wisconsin was a paper organization whose candidates always finished third, behind the Republican and Progressive Party nominees. But in 1940, organized labor was not solid for Roosevelt, due to infiltration by the Communists into the new CIO unions. The Germans, who normally voted Republican or Progressive, stayed away from the Roosevelt banner. Roosevelt's eventual narrow victory in the state was due to the Wisconsin voters of the La Follette breed, plus a shift of normally Republican or Progressive Scandinavian voters to the Roosevelt line on the interventionist issue.

Michigan had never quite divorced itself from the Republican ties which had kept it in line for ninety years preceding the New Deal. The birthplace of the Republican Party, it had been a supporter rivalled only by Pennsylvania, Vermont and Maine in its faithfulness. While it voted for Roosevelt in 1932 in revolt against the Hoover Depression, and again in 1936 in approval of the New Deal, it reacted against the labor troubles in the steel and auto plants during Roosevelt's second term.

The new technique of sit-down strikes, accompanied by bloody rioting, cost the Democrats votes among Michigan's middle class.

There were French-Canadians along the border, normally Republican, who voted for Roosevelt in 1940, but not enough to overcome the isolationist voters and the people troubled by labor's new activity. So Michigan's substantial bloc of electoral votes went into Willkie's pocket, though by the slenderest of margins of any of the battleground states.

A recapitulation of the vote follows:

			Majority	
State	Roosevelt	Willkie	Roosevelt	Willkie
Maine	156,478	165,951		9,473
New Hampshire	125,292	110,127	15,165	
Vermont	64,269	78,371		14,102
Massachusetts	1,076,552	939,700	136,852	
Connecticut	417,621	361,021	56,600	
Rhode Island	182,132	132,653	49,479	
New York	3,251,918	3,027,478	224,440	
Pennsylvania	2,171,035	1,889,848	281,187	
New Jersey	1,016,404	944,876	71,528	
Ohio	1,733,139	1,586,773	146,366	
Indiana	874,073	899,466		25,393
Illinois	2,149,934	2,047,240	102,690	
Wisconsin	704,281	679,260	25,021	
Michigan	1,032,991	1,039,917		6,926
Totals	14,956,119	13,902,681	1,109,328	55,894

Thus it can be seen that Roosevelt had an edge of somewhat more than a million out of nearly twenty-nine million votes in the decisive region. The hope that Willkie could win them over, with no one else likely to do so, had been the rationale of the Willkie nomination. The inherent fault in the approach lay in the fact that he needed victory not only in the region as a whole, but in every one of its component states.

12 The Coda

There is no convenient place in the American political system for either ex-Presidents or ex-nominees for the Presidency. Ex-Presidents get expenses to pay staff for the handling of their mail; the chairmanship of large committees operating in the field of kind thoughts and public welfare; and a kind of ex-officio respect they may or may not have enjoyed while in the thick of things. Politically they are dead ducks.

Not one in modern times has had any measure of control over his own party once he left office. When Harry S Truman, the most politically-minded ex-President, was still in the White House in 1952, he was able to swing convention delegates behind Adlai Stevenson as his potential successor. Four years later when he tried to make Averell Harriman the nominee instead of giving Stevenson a second try, Truman found he controlled no delegates at all.

Men who were nominees for the Presidency and were defeated have no status ex-officio. The man himself may believe that having been his party's nominee for President makes him its leader until the next nominating convention has been held. But unless he has a continuing hold on the party's rank and file of the kind that could secure him the nomination as a new contender for it, he is just a has-been and also-ran.

The national parties really come into being only for the period of presidential elections. The national chairman, expected to run the party machinery between presidential elections, is for the losing side always a temporary phenomenon—the personal choice and campaign manager of the convention nominee. After the nominee has been defeated, the national chairman either resigns gracefully or is ousted by pressure from rival factions any time from six months to a year following the election.

Control of party policies and machinery then returns to the congressional leadership—if it has any stature—or flows back to the fifty state organizations which make up the national party at presidential election time.

Up to 1940, the only man who had successfully bucked the system was William Jennings Bryan. Others since who achieved some measure of success were Stevenson, Dewey and Nixon. Willkie sought to do the same after his 1940 defeat. It is well known that he forced his party a long way toward internationalism, though the leadership and much of the rank and file rejected his bid for a second nomination.

What is much less recognized is that Willkie carried on, after his defeat, a relationship with the man who defeated him for President that was—and still is—unique in American politics. For a period of two years following the 1940 election, Wendell Willkie worked hand-in-glove with Franklin Delano Roosevelt, primarily in the areas of national defense and global affairs, but also on the domestic political level.

Some indications of their relationship were available at the time, but much of their teamwork, and the results of it, was never publicized and was therefore all the more effective. No President in office had ever before worked either publicly or privately with his previous opponent. Herbert Hoover, after his defeat in 1932, tried to work out a joint responsibility arrangement with FDR to cover the interim between election and inauguration, but Roosevelt avoided it.

Earlier, in World War I, Teddy Roosevelt pressed with boyish enthusiasm the idea that he should raise and command a division of American volunteers for service in France, the way he had led a regiment in the Spanish-American War. Wilson coldly rejected it. The Willkie program, also the product of national crisis, was completely mature and so was Franklin Roosevelt's way of working it out.

The post-election arrangements between Roosevelt and Willkie grew out of Willkie's behavior in accepting defeat. It was apparent by ten o'clock election night that Willkie had lost. By midnight Lem Jones, Willkie's press secretary, was being bombarded with pressure for a concession by the candidate. McNary, the vice-presidential nominee, had already issued his own concession without checking with Willkie.

Willkie did not expect to win. He told Jones while the polls were still open on Election Day that he did not believe in miracles. That night he told Jones he would withhold his statement because he had some things to say that would go beyond the normal concession of defeat and the sending of congratulations to the winner. He did not want his thinking lost in the thunder of the morning-after returns.

After he slept on it, he realized that he still had not put his ideas into appropriate language. He had Jones arrange for radio time on a national hookup for the following Monday night, November 11. At the same time he sent off to Roosevelt a more than usually warm message. It read:

> Congratulations on your re-election as President of the United States. I know we are both gratified that so many American citizens participated in the election. I wish you all personal health and happiness. Cordially, Wendell Willkie.

Roosevelt's reply was on the same plane:

> Please accept my sincerest thanks on your message of congratulations. I greatly appreciate the assurance of your good wishes for my health and happiness, which I heartily reciprocate. Franklin D. Roosevelt.

Willkie's Monday night radio speech, carried by every network, was aimed at toning down the bitterness that still existed among the Roosevelt-haters who had supported Willkie's candidacy as the opportunity to get "That Man" out of the White House, and thus to unify the nation for the crises still ahead.

Willkie went into the fact that the American political system does not allow for governments of national unity, with coalition cabinets; that under our system any Republican who entered the Roosevelt Administration did so as a Presidential subordinate, not as a coequal representing the other major party. But that did not mean, he argued, that the Republicans had to oppose everything Roosevelt did, to play politics as though no crisis existed.

He said:

> Although constitutional government had been blotted out elsewhere, here in America men and women kept it triumphantly alive. No matter which side you were on, this great expression of faith in the free system of government must have given hope wherever man hopes to be free.
>
> People became bitter. Many things were said which in calmer moments might have been left unsaid or might have been worded more thoughtfully. There is no bitterness in my heart; I hope there is none in yours.
>
> We have elected Franklin D. Roosevelt President. He is your President. He is my President. We all owe him the respect due to his high office, we will support him with our best efforts for our country. And we will pray God may guide his hand during the next four years in administering the affairs of the people.
>
> A vital element in the balanced operation of democracy is a strong, alert and watchful opposition. That is our task for the next four years. We must constitute ourselves a vigorous, loyal and public-spirited opposition.

Roosevelt had always liked Willkie, whom he had met during the TVA fight over the Commonwealth and Southern properties, and he was quick to act on Willkie's offer of cooperation. Intimates of Willkie recall that there were a number of calls from the White House to Willkie in New York, after which Willkie would board a late afternoon or early evening plane for Washington. He would be met at the airport by an unmarked White House car, which left him off at the back entrance to the President's mansion. After the talk with the President, he would be taken back to the airport and be at his desk the next morning, with the same measures of secrecy used.

There is no record of these trips, but the best information is that they began before Roosevelt sent his lend-lease program to Congress on January 10, 1941. Roosevelt desperately needed Republican support for lend-lease, and Willkie gave it to him.

The program itself stripped the United States of even technical neutrality in the European war. Britain had run out of cash to pay for matériel of war and for food; it had even liquidated and used up all private British investment money here. If it did not get food and ammunition and ships to carry both, it would have been starved out of the war as effectively as if it were bombed out or overrun by an invading German army. But U.S. law, even apart from neutrality acts, barred war credits here for any nation which had defaulted on World War I loans. Britain had done so when Germany's reparations to it were halted in 1930.

Willkie agreed to support the lend-lease idea, which scrapped all previous statutory bars, and took the dollar sign off the aid we were giving Britain. Roosevelt compared lend-lease—in a press conference preceding the introduction of the legislation—to lending a neighbor one's fire hose to put out a fire that threatened his home and might also threaten one's own. All we would want later would be the return of the hose, Roosevelt said.

The Republican leadership in Congress and elsewhere teamed up with Democratic isolationists like Burton K. Wheeler to denounce lend-lease as just another Rooseveltian stride toward involving the nation in war.

Willkie, whose statement in support of lend-lease was issued two days after the bill was introduced, sent telegrams to every member of Congress saying that "the problem is not how to keep America out of the war, but how to keep the war out of

America," a total adoption of Roosevelt's theory that we were protecting ourselves by supporting Britain.

Even before the alliance of Roosevelt and Willkie on lend-lease, the two cooperated on a Willkie mission to Britain. Willkie, in the course of writing a magazine article on American aid to Britain, realized he had no first-hand knowledge of what was going on at the receiving end. Roosevelt not only assented to the trip—State Department approval was necessary for an American citizen to enter a war zone—but gave Willkie, publicly, a warm letter of introduction to Winston Churchill. Privately, he discussed with him what Willkie could do and how he could do it to further stimulate American support of the aid-to-Britain program.

After Willkie returned from his highly successful London trip—during which he toured the bombed docks and dwellings and reported freely to the press his impressions of the gallant British resistance—Willkie and Roosevelt continued to meet. And they worked out a program under which the President and his recent opponent alternated in taking public positions on defense matters.

The question of convoys—which would take our naval ships into the war zone infested by German submarines—was a very touchy one. Willkie took the lead on that by demanding convoys to make sure that the goods and arms we were producing and "lending" Britain were not sunk en route. Roosevelt, probably by prearrangement with Willkie, did not go as far as Willkie demanded. He moved American troops into Iceland, more than halfway across the North Atlantic, established an American "defense" base there, and announced that our naval ships would convoy the goods that far. This cut to less than half the segment of the North Atlantic that the British had to protect with their Navy.

Another time, Willkie asked for the removal from the book of every section of our old Neutrality Act. Roosevelt followed again with a lesser step, the repeal of the sections that prohibited our arming our merchant ships. Roosevelt was extremely careful in not stepping too far ahead of American public opinion at any time, and there is no doubt that Willkie acted as a pace-setter with the President's blessings, even at his request.

In August, 1942, Willkie and a small group of friends took off in an Army bomber for a trip around the world, which Roosevelt sponsored by giving Willkie the rank of his personal ambassador. This was a typical Rooseveltian gesture, to use someone close to give him a personal report on things he couldn't see for himself, and to make sure that State Department red tape didn't stand in his emissary's way.

On the trip, Willkie crossed the South Atlantic from Brazil to the African Gold Coast, went from there to the Near East—in time to announce with General Montgomery the victory at El Alemein—and thence into Russia, where he dined and wined with Stalin. He later met with Marshal Chiang Kai-shek in Chungking before completing his circumnavigation of the globe, 31,000 miles in 49 days.

Willkie had Roosevelt's permission to go anyplace but India, which at that time was still unsuccessfully seeking its independence of Britain. Roosevelt knew that Churchill was extremely sensitive about India, reacting violently to American sympathies for Indian independence. He also knew how Willkie felt on the subject. When Willkie, in Chungking, predicted as well as called for the end of all colonialism after the war, Roosevelt publicly tsk-tsked at Willkie's stand, though he privately agreed with him. Again, Roosevelt and Willkie were acting as silent partners.

One of the things that extended their working together in international affairs to domestic politics was their mutual distaste for Tom Dewey. In the spring of 1942 Dewey, who had gone to the 1940 convention with more delegates than anyone else, was an obvious leading contender for the 1944 nomination. His first major step toward that nomination would be his nomination and election as Governor of New York in the fall of 1942, which seemed very likely unless the Democrats could come up with a strong candidate to succeed Herbert Lehman, retiring after four terms.

Both Roosevelt as a New York Democrat and Willkie as a Republican presidential aspirant were interested in seeing that Dewey was not elected Governor.

Willkie could not go out after the Republican nomination for Governor—although some of his friends publicly urged that he do so—because Dewey had complete control of the New York State organization. To oppose Dewey in the primary and lose—as he was certain to do under the system of selecting state convention delegates—would eliminate Willkie himself as a presidential contender two years later.

Willkie quietly opposed Dewey's selection by conversations with his friends in Republican circles, even presenting the publishers of the *New York Herald Tribune*, the leading Republican organ with evidence that Dewey was making internationalist speeches publicly and isolationist speeches privately.

At Roosevelt's suggestion, Willkie slipped out to a *New York Times* reporter whom he trusted the story—which both he and Roosevelt wanted printed—that Owen D. Young, a very respectable industrialist as well as philanthropist, was being considered by Roosevelt as the best man the Democrats could nominate to defeat Dewey. But Roosevelt did not control the New York State Democratic organization—Jim Farley did—and the trial balloon had no effect.

After 1942, Roosevelt and Willkie saw less of each other for two reasons. First, Roosevelt no longer needed outside support for his foreign policies, the attack by the Japanese at Pearl Harbor on December 7, 1941, having ended the debate here.

Second, Willkie was beginning to emerge as an active seeker for himself of the Republican nomination for President in 1944. Continued close association with Roosevelt was potentially awkward for both if the war lasted long enough for Roosevelt to seek a fourth term.

Willkie's stand on lend-lease had split him away from the

Republican leaders in Congress. His appeal for the party to be the party of the Loyal Opposition, supporting the President, was treason to the diehards; his trip around the world marked him as a Presidential agent seeking to reinfiltrate the Republican Party, so there was little chance Willkie could get renominated. He was defeated in the Wisconsin primary in 1944, withdrew from the race, and Governor Dewey of New York was an easy winner at the Republican National Convention over Govenor John W. Bricker of Ohio.

Thereafter there were a number of emissaries from Roosevelt to Willkie endeavoring to set up, at Roosevelt's request, further meetings of the two. Willkie stalled, feeling that they represented an attempt to get Willkie on Roosevelt's side in the campaign the latter would be waging against Dewey. There were also notes back and forth, some of which leaked to the press from the White House end, others that never saw the light of day.

Roosevelt is known to have discussed the idea of he and Willkie teaming up after the war to head a new liberal party, with all the conservatives and isolationists on the other side; he is reported, by Ellsworth Barnard in his *Wendell Willkie, Fighter for Freedom,* as having considered Willkie the man to head up postwar reconstruction in Europe. Willkie died on October 8, 1944, before any of these plans could even be aired, and before he even took a position on the 1944 campaign. He did pledge Ray Baldwin, sent to him by Dewey as a Republican emissary, that he would not come out for Roosevelt. Other acts indicated quite as clearly that he would not support Dewey. He apparently planned to just "sit that one out."

In any event, there was a close enough relationship between Roosevelt and Willkie to lead Robert Sherwood to write of it as follows in his *Roosevelt and Hopkins:*

> It was my belief in 1943 and early in 1944 that if Willkie were to win the Republican nomination, Roosevelt would not run for a fourth term. I had no tangible basis for that

belief, and it was a double hypothetical surmise because it was evident for a long time to Roosevelt that Willkie had no chance whatever of being nominated.

Sherwood, at the time constantly in and out of the White House as a leading member of Roosevelt's final speechwriting team, was in a position to witness the birth and growth of a political relationship as unique as the circumstances under which they both had come to contest the Presidency in the great campaign of 1940.